ESTHER RAM

THE SILLY
THING

Shaping the Story
of Life & Death

FREE ASSOCIATION BOOKS

First published in 2020 by
Free Association Books

A CIP Catalogue of this book is available from
the British Library

ISBN: 978-1-9113834-4-4

Cover designed and typeset by
www.chandlerbookdesign.com

Printed and bound in Great Britain by
Biddles Books Ltd.

1

PREFACE

A s I write this preface, we are in the third week of the UK Lockdown in response to the invisible threat of the coronavirus that plagues the countries of our world. To some extent, the fear of death, ordinarily split off from our conscious minds, has come so close that we imagine its ominous message entering into our homes, through opened letterboxes and in the packaging of food deliveries.

At first, many in the Western world sat back and watched with a degree of complacency, situating the human devastation of the virus in China; a thick-skinned narcissistic position. They projected the reality of our vulnerable, fragile existences, and located it far from our shores resorting to a 'them and us' narrative that both generates and, arguably, follows from a racist state of mind.

With a government that has, historically, given dependency, decay and death a bad name, and has eroded those systems that support precarious lives with systematic under-resourcing, it is no wonder a strict and enforced lockdown has taken its time here. In the UK, myths about our island-like, independent robustness circulate as if we are immune to the contagion of dying, but of course, this is a fundamental aspect of the human condition. Certainly, with this ever-spreading viral Other, some levelling out is taking place, a sense that we can – as was always the case – all be taken by death at any point; there is no scope for humiliation now. On April 5th 2020, even our prime minister is currently under hospital care.

Yet we know that doctors, nurses, health care assistants – those on the frontline of this epidemic – are likely to encounter higher loads of the virus,, and will die. While we applaud them on our streets at 8pm each Thursday, a moment of joyous collaboration and a symbol of gratitude, we may also discover a sense of grievance that these most essential of workers have been let down time and time again by a divisive ideology that creates chasms and inequities between weak and strong; poor and rich. This sense of grievance (Hoggett, 2010), if harnessed, might prevent us from forgetting the learning of the epidemic; it might prevent us from wishing, from the relative comfort of our protective online office-bedrooms, to resume life as before. Now we can see the real, brutal impact of what it means when those that do the hands-on caring are not well cared for themselves.

And so, while we might begin to have some understanding of what it is like to live with a much greater awareness of our own mortality (a catalyst for transformation, no doubt), and the possible endpoints of those we love, we will also see the shocking social inequities of our society with more clarity and, one hopes, greater empathy. Women (or men) behind closed doors, fearing for their lives in a different way, shut in with their persecutors in the most intensely holed-up situation; children without gardens, without food; those struggling without nature's song; self-esteem plummeting for those without work, rampant fears about social deaths and crumbling identities. The future for many looks bleak. This is about survival, about the realities of lives with basic needs unfulfilled, very little opportunity to learn something from the epidemic of fear that runs alongside the viral one; very little time, or space, to apply the thinking of philosophers and psychologists in reflecting upon our death anxiety and creating meaning therein.

For others, those who like to think, to write, to reflect, and who are able to do so because work continues to come, food is available, a home with minimal tension... then perhaps more scope exists to ruminate on possibilities. We might take the imaginative leap and mull over what the dying have often taught us; that in the face of life's impending conclusion, there can be a quality to each day that can be more meaningful; that pleasure can be found in the adaptation to a slower, simpler pace, that we rarely need as much as we might want, and that human connection – one which offers closeness and space simultaneously - is vital to our sense of continued being.

In the therapeutic community, this recognition of the importance of the relational field has been made manifest by the anxious, and active, springing up of Zoom, Skype, Google hangout groups. These all provide a necessary, supportive meeting place in which the rampant projections and raw, panicked, angry, painful feelings can be processed among trusting others. For many therapists, transitioning to mediated therapy – adapting to new spaces which may, at times, hinder relational depth, but at others lead to the discovery of a different and powerful dynamic in the therapeutic alliance – these spaces, these communities of emotional and intellectual collaboration, also lead to thoughts of the possibility for a more cohesive society, one embedded in love; a relational activism that may challenge our former and normativising discourses of separation, competition and individualism. It's hard not to imagine, to desire, a future such as this.

For those of us working psychotherapeutically in palliative care, our organisations themselves are gripped with the fear of occupational death, a crises about funding presents itself: hospice provision is only partly funded by the government (in England this approximates to around 32% of the income is statutory funding), yet 225, 000 people receive palliative care support each year and 72,000 access bereavement care following a death (Hospice UK, 2020). Currently, the hospice sector is engaged in the corona relief effort and many of its doctors and nurses are supporting the NHS as it swells and bulges with haunting cases. A government bailout is perhaps long overdue, as is the PPE that is finally becoming available.

Psychotherapists in this field are hearing stories daily of harrowing, abrupt, traumatic deaths before their time, stories of friends and families unable to soothe those that are dying with touch, or with presence, or with gentle words. Patients are dying behind closed doors, with professionals shielded in masks. Deaths have been live-streamed here as they have been in Italy's Bergamo, with parting words spoken on Facetimes; funerals delayed, barely attended. The marking of lives once lived, are on hold. The impact of confused, complex grief is likely to be felt in most communities, and the bereaved will unlikely have those images of a peaceful well-supported death which my father and I experienced with Mum. Those dying from Covid19 may have struggled to say goodbye, hands will not be held, there will have been minimal time for considered advanced care plans and the laudable policy ideal of 'choice'.

We hear also of people already living with terrifying life limiting diseases who are now in lockdown, wondering what their lives have become, with the prospect of dying alone; a double layer of persecution; We hear of families circumventing the necessary severity of lockdown by appearing at windows on the birthdays of parents that are unlikely to see another year, and of singing at the tops of their voices to bring gifts that are wrapped in thought and time; some delivering news that babies too might be born – as a way, you might imagine – of making sure the family system goes-on-being.

The work of psychotherapy in this context is heavier still. The reassurance of the physical presence of client and therapist is out of reach, and each week you are concerned that another person with a terminal condition, whom you meet regularly, might have died before their time. We sense the staff team's overwhelm, those critical of tears in clinical supervision now weeping into their hands when they see a pet by the side of a corpse, whining in the lifelessness of the room, at the still hospital bed.

But with all this desperation the care provided continues to be as tender as it can be, and this is in spite of the sense of distance, in spite of the (shamefully articulated) moments of suspicion between workers and patients alike – a fear that one or the other might be carrying these viral balls of club-shaped spikes and may cause further breathlessness in those already breathless, from anxiety, or from illness, or professional pressure.

Of course, in among the reality of this external pestilence – the virus itself, the cracks in our infrastructure, the revelations of poverty and despair – and the epidemics of splitting, and of suspicion which we can succumb to internally, there is also an incredible recognition of the life force, a recognition of the human spirit, and of man's search for continued meaning of the type Viktor Frankl writes. Those with COPD, of cancers of the blood, of tumours behind the eyes and nasal cavities, of MS and MND – bodies already in full, inescapable lock-down –

may continue to tell us that to look out unto the skies and to see
the birds continue to fly is privilege enough; to touch the soil
with bare hands and to plant alongside a child or spouse brings
immediate comfort. Not only, in this context, am I continuing
to learn from people who are dying but, among other therapists
and with palliative care professionals, regular online meets have
become an important site of community. In these groups, we
share our deep concerns yet also laugh with each other, which
lightens the load and validates our relatedness as a people in the
pool of humanity, particles of a universe that will always be in
flux. It is in these anchoring moments where we might begin
to recognise that we need each other's care – always - in order
to steady ourselves. As has always been the way...

April 2020

INTRODUCTION

*'Like everyone else, I am incapable of conceiving
infinity; and yet I do not accept finity.'*
Simone de Beauvoir (1972)

From the age of nine, I began to understand that my life would have an endpoint, and I would find myself sitting on the wall outside our home looking up at the sky and the stars beyond, weighing up my significance, or lack of it, in relation to the mightiness of the planet that I found myself in. Thoughts about death and dying have stayed with me as I have aged, often lingering in the background of my decisions about which path to take in life. This is not to say that when making choices I have always managed successfully to refer back to what is arguably a philosophical frame related to meaning and finitude since sometimes the unconscious has overruled all rational thought and, like most of us, wild mess has ensued. That said, the question of who we are and what we become has challenged me for many years now, as it has challenged many others, great thinkers and everyday people such as me. As a result I have been driven to get closer to ageing and to death partially because of a residual anxiety about time running out and partially because somewhere, in the depths of my mind, I have known that working with and caring for those who are gradually unbecoming can provide one of the richest sites of learning. Learning, that is, about what it might be to be human and to exist alongside others; learning what is important and what may be a distraction from living; and learning that in any one of us the complexity, the paradoxes, the sheer number of layers we have is confusing and yet, in exploring them, we might find some tentative, yet changing, clarity about the poetry of who we are. This is most certainly the experience I have had in working psychotherapeutically with those who are dying, and their families and friends living with grief.

It is widely thought that the West has been in a state of 'death denial', though more recently it has been argued that we have been moving into a period of 'death revival' (Clarke, 2018). Whether this shift is actually taking place at a profound ontological level I do not know, but faced as we are with the impending existential threat brought about by the planetary emergency, it does become apparent that there is a pervasive split between those defensively in denial of climate change and those who are mobilising their ongoing grief, the anguish of potential and further ecological loss, into active engagement.

Another narrative is also emerging at this time. In January 2018, Maria Meltzer of the *Guardian* reported that death was becoming cool, the headline supported by the image of a skull in shades seducing its readers. With the advent of death cafes, alternative green funerals, celebrations of death around the world such as the Dia de Los Muertos, the latter of which has arguably been co-opted in the UK and America for commercial gain, there is a sense that speaking about death more openly is becoming *de rigueur*. And while there is something to be said for integrating death into the everyday, rather than being split off from ordinary life, death is, quite simply, not cool. This semantics of consumerism overlooks the anguish of people who are dying, the deliberate effort of grace it takes to meet each day with a life-limiting condition, the pain and sadness of those who are bereaved and the reality of the mess, the courage, both emotional and physical, as the body and mind disintegrate. Writing in his final weeks with motor neurone disease, Joe Hammond (2019) encapsulates the agonising tension between recognising the beauty of simple existence and the pain of further withdrawing and disconnecting from it:

> I can't be active in the life of my children. I have to see what the day brings. There was the moment last week when Tom rested his cheek into my upper arm, gently twisted the top of his head upwards against my flesh like a nestling cat, then twirled away. It was a moment that must have lasted five seconds at most but I kept it with me – held on to it – for days, as if I wasn't just making contact, but taking an imprint... I'm very still with this disease now: I'm an observer, sensing lives happening in other rooms. I hear bottles and cans rattling in plastic bags. I see the rain at three o'clock on a Sunday. All this detail goes by or around me and I see it working. I see three people moving and turning together – and it's no longer breaking my heart. It's just sad and comforting. I didn't expect the end of my life to feel like the future... It's really hard to cry when you rely on a mask for air.
>
> **(14 DECEMBER 2019, *GUARDIAN*)**

Of course, we might surmise that in rampant individualistic societies, death has been denied so that we can be conned into the fantasy of building permanence through the purchase of goods, objects, houses, branded fixed identities that we convince ourselves will not fade with the test of time. But deep down we know this to be a falsity: we are changing and dying in every moment. As philosophers, spiritual masters and great writers have noted throughout time, to flee from the reality of our certain death is to avoid thinking at any depth about the lives we live. Seneca, the Buddha, Heidegger – to name a few – advocated a sort of living-in-the-face-of-death, to live each moment as if it were our last, to discover our own authenticity in the present moment with the ongoing knowledge that in the final breath the meaning of our lives would be summed up. And yet at the same time, these lofty ideals, which are of course so rich, valuable and thought-provoking, may not always be the concern of those who are genuinely struggling to live each day; who work in the squalid heat of landfill sites trying to find scraps to sell; or who prostitute themselves in order to survive. But some of us are not in those unenviable positions and perhaps, for us, the duty is to use the recognition of our own temporality, making our lives purposeful, useful, in some small way, in the service of this wondrous planet and those whom we live alongside. And through this process, no doubt, we are also giving ourselves an existential gift, which is priceless.

What follows is the story of my own mother's experience of dying, a short struggle with an unexpected glioblastoma – the most aggressive form of brain cancer – that took away her capacity for language, and forced her into a glazed world of suspended time. She was not an exceptional person who will leave her trace in the annals of history – no published sonnets, paintings hung in galleries, songs written – but she was a woman of remarkable fortitude in the face of death; at a time when our politics distances itself from empathetic understanding and drives forth a narrative of separation, and intolerance, I like to think that her death, and the death of many of the people I have worked with, leave behind both a lesson and a story of simple humanity.

Apart from the unfolding of my mother's brain cancer, none of the vignettes included in these pages are based on individual people; rather they are representative of the kinds and complexities of human experiences that psychotherapists work with in palliative care. These vignettes have been italicised throughout the book to make it clear that they are fictionalised accounts, hence the short narratives are not referenced with a date or name.

However, I am deeply grateful to all the people with whom I have had the privilege of being alongside in the course of prolonged and painful illnesses, who continue to teach me where meanings can be discovered and re-discovered; and with the many bereaved people who continue to share their stories and deepest intimacies, as well as the members of staff who work frontline and who are able to summon compassion and tendernesses, when society as a whole tends to overlook just how valuable their contribution is.

In every encounter with patients, families and staff teams, embedded as they often are in meaningful, trusting connection, I have often walked away inspired, taken aback and having learned so much about how straightforward and yet how profound we humans are; often, as a result of all of these relationships, a therapist's eyes become more open to the possibilities of life – and the ways we might manage to live it.

DIAGNOSIS

*'I cannot think of death as more than the going
out of one room into another.'*

William Black (1826)

On Christmas Day 2017, on my husband Matt's
suggestion, we bought my mother a dictaphone to
record her memories and her life. Having taught
English for many years in several large comprehensive schools,
and being a relentless storyteller and chatterbox, Joyce Margaret
Jones had a lot to say. It was, perhaps he thought, a way
in to all those thoughts, feelings, experiences stored in that
churning mind of hers; she often remained stoically silent in
the nineteenth-century cottage that she shared with my father,
a seeker of solitude.

On Boxing Day 2018, Mum was rushed into hospital, having
lost her speech, mumbling semblances of words that had once
so easily flowed from her. During that dislocating, jumbled
time where words combined with other words to form sounds

that no one around her could comprehend, one thing was clear and she repeated it with whatever half-words she could: this woman, with her determined, forceful spirit, did not want to survive without language. Though noises came, she had been rendered voiceless and misunderstood by a three x two centimetre glioblastoma that was growing in her left temporal lobe. This had frightened her beyond all measure. It was not the possibility of death that she feared, but time imprisoned in a mind that had no outlet; where people look on and attempt, if you're lucky, to fill in your gaps; or, if you're unlucky, rush on, unhearing, making incorrect assumptions that don't belong.

For the weeks that she stayed in different wards in different hospitals, waiting for some further clarity on her diagnosis, my father, husband and I rushed around, buying new nighties, slippers for wide swollen feet, high protein nutritional drinks to bring back appetite and taste. In times when crisis punctures the seemingly mundane certainties of the everyday, we try to take back control, to fix any little thing that might be fixable, bringing comfort where little can be found. It was as if we had stopped thinking, becoming automata, doers, operating on high-speed; it was hard to slow down, yet the visits to my mother demanded a slower pace, a more watchful, reflective presence to try to hear about the nightmares and hallucinations she was having, the fears of not getting out, the cuddles that she needed – from all of us.

Gradually, words came back with the steroid, Dexamethasone, and attentive nursing care which my mother received during her stay in three different hospitals. So, as I write this, I am able to stand in my mother's house, wearing my mother's knitwear, enjoying her voice and speech again.

As I sit next to her, reflecting on the strange links and connections that are made between people, and over our lifetimes,

I realise it is time to make use of that dictaphone presciently bought for Mum that Christmas. We can only hope that any recordings will allow us all to find her voice on those days that we might fear we are losing it, to hear her, to take in those wise thoughts that light up the brain even in the darkest of times.

As a psychotherapist working in palliative care, I am often struck by the way in which those of us working in this field might occasionally become the keepers of life stories, hidden secret parts of a person's history. It seemed that I would always regret it if Mum had wanted to share some of her life with me, and if I failed to make myself available to hearing it. My father had done something similar with his own mother, who was born within the sound of Bow Bells and who later moved to the valleys of Wales as the wife of a Calvinist Methodist minister. He had collected a life-time of stories that she had shared with him over several months, which he had made into a booklet for the extended Welsh family: a combination of personal and social history, interspersed with my grandmother's fervent religious beliefs that generally seemed to help her as she journeyed through the bewildering maze of Alzheimer's disease a short time later.

Psychotherapy is in part about the human story, and the way we attribute meaning to the complex multi-layered narratives of linear and spatial time. The writer and critic, Alison Light (2019), once married to radical historian of the British Left Raphael Samuel, notes in her scholarly and deeply touching memoir how she had tried to interview her husband.

> As oral history it was a failure. Raphael was keen on my speaking as much as he did and on the tape we interrupt each other freely, calling each other 'darling', hardly the model of professionalism. I began conventionally enough

with childhood memories, as if we had all the time in the
world to work our leisurely way towards young adulthood
and later life. (p. 158)

Light (2019) had also studied and been involved in the
practice and receipt of therapy, one to one and in groups, at the
Institute of Group Analysis. Her fascination, we might imagine,
was also with the meaning of relating and the unfolding of
narrative. Mine too, and yet similarly keeping any kind of
professionalism with one's mother is nigh on impossible: in
the midst of our conversations she would call me 'artichoke
heart', 'aubergine' – revealing both her love of cooking and
her sentimentalism – and I too would giggle on tape, or ask a
leading question of my own interest. Most unnerving, though,
like Light (2019), is that strange belief that there is 'all the time
in the world' to get to things – with Mum, there was not. We had
a month, perhaps, of verbal fluency, and thereafter the words and
phrases stumbled upon one another and at times ended up in a
heap of something barely decipherable. And so, to understand
Mum, even the most mundane of her communications, one of
us had to be with her, reading the facial expressions, the way
her hands gestured, the nods or shakes, the growls.

There are pockets of skin on Mum's face, which belong to
a much younger woman, and her eyes, when she makes a point
she herself approves of, glisten into life. It seems that there are
times, following the crazy, earth-shattering news of a cancer
diagnosis (or of any other terminal illness), that we might begin
to capture and to see those we love in their full intensity.

It is a strange thing to have become a psychotherapist in
palliative care, and to understand so deeply as I write this
that we can be at our most vital in the midst of desperate
impending pain. As I sit on Mum's bed, her brain intact, having

left hospital without a resection of the damaged area, a yellow fleece blanket covering her legs stitched with a message that our children chose – 'Mama, we love you', – she pipes up, her words absolute, unequivocal:

> 'Life's a funny business.' She pauses. 'What you have that's got anything good... hold on, hold on. Never get rid of it and learn to appreciate just what you've got. I don't think people do that enough... I really don't think people do anymore. They think they can chuck and go and get a new this or that but it doesn't give you happiness or joy.'

My mother has known experiences that were not good, and so I listen carefully. This is not some new age philosophy here. This is the wisdom of a woman whose childhood was a place of constant drama, so it is not unsurprising that she sounds theatrical in her truisms.

> 'And when all is said and done I am absolutely convinced that love and joy are the most important things in existence, more than anything else in this world. And giving and sharing are the most important things in life, beyond a shadow of a doubt – your children will benefit because they will have a strong base. So important.'

My mother's bases were not always strong, and, though she was cared for by her own mother, she has lived a life informed by the lingering fragility of an inner child exposed to violence and to precariousness. My mum is no Melanie Klein or D.W. Winnicott, but her intuition is a tool she has used throughout her life. One day – I am not sure when – I will very much miss it; that instantaneous way she sums up situations and people; their ambivalences, muddles and confusions. All from a woman whose brain is now very much letting her down.

She continues, and I am surprised that this growth, with its tendrils and tentacles, is invading her thinking space because what she says is not just a muttering, a reflection, it is full of the social and the political, too. And bloody hell, she, my mum, is very much here. No sign yet of giving up.

> 'I just don't know why we have lost those messages. It's greed. Because it is greed. This is one of the things that have destroyed, or are destroying the beauty of our humanity. I am sure of it. I am sure of it. And yet,' she says, noting the strange revolutions many of us human beings make each day, 'you have all these nurses and all those doctors giving, giving, giving...'

In the two hospitals she stayed in as they tried to make a diagnosis, she looked around each day and pointed out the multiple nationalities that support our NHS; she considered the care of the nursing staff, the way they sat and chatted with her when they could; the quiet patience, yet humble shadow-like figures of the domestics; the doctor, a little awkward, with sometimes potted English that understood she did not want a life without access to language. She noticed them all.

> '... and I don't know if they are appreciated enough.'

She says this to me, someone who works among professionals of a similar ilk, in a similar care environment, and we both know there is some truth in this. And we are both, on this day, very much speaking the same language. What Mum had noticed in her stays in several hospitals was the attentiveness of staff, who were clearly under inordinate pressure to meet the needs of patients, sometimes with the added complexity of having to respond to antagonistic, abusive behaviours, as well as dealing with a rush of emergencies which come with little warning. Though she was often impatient to return home, Mum always seemed curious about the stories of lives unfolding on the ward; a veritable nosey-parker. During her stays in hospital, she had made friends with a Russian woman (both of them without a full complement of English vocabulary), another woman interested in poetry, a girl whose experience of institutional care and shaming meant that she was always on the attack. What Mum always talked about, though, was the care, the humaneness she felt she was in receipt of. Somehow, in her garbled speech, as it was then, in the shock and numbness of the crisis she had survived, she tirelessly spoke of staff whom she felt able to trust, and what a difference this made to a woman who had prided herself on her very singular sense of resilience and independence. These people respected Mum in her moments of dependency; in those momentary interactions on the ward, they never shamed into silencing her voice or her being. Like others that she observed, she was held in mind in the most human of ways even at those times when the system, the scheduling, the procedures were unable to provide a structural container for patient anxiety.

Yet the presence of basic humanity is not often captured by policymakers. It stands to reason, then, that I have sympathy for Hoggett's (2009) argument that, 'Western democracies have given rise to narcissistic [achievement-oriented] cultures that are in flight from dependency and the acceptance of human limits' (p. 164). For him, those who construct policy often express an intolerance of dependency; an attempt perhaps to tidy up human vulnerabilities and suffering (Froggett, 2002; Hoggett, 2009). Service users are conceptualised as rational decision-makers whose needs will be met through the provision of outcome-focused services, responding within reasonable timescales. As a result only a 'thin' (Froggett, 2002) conception of human need is acknowledged which turns a blind eye to the importance of being known, recognised. Hoggett (2009) states that:

> . . . new technologies of performativity have created a thick skin… that mediates between the state and its managers and policy makers on the one hand and the many victims of social suffering characteristic of increasingly socially polarized democracies under the conditions of neoliberal globalisation on the other. (p. 169)

This thick skin seems impervious to the emotional cost of facing greater dependency, death and decline, and social policy peddles a fantasy that such anxieties can be better assuaged by efficiently performing services than through compassionate micro-interactions between people. Now that Mum was clearly very poorly, she understood the value of such encounters and wanted to repeat her findings to anyone who would listen.

———————

After some weeks at home, following the initial crisis, we visit the hospital for a second time. An appointment has been scheduled to see the neurosurgeon, a man with a warm open face. You can tell he likes people by the way he introduces himself. This is not a man who elevates himself; rather he makes every effort to meet his patients as if they are visitors to his home. I get the impression he likes my mother, her warm face and smile mirroring his. He asks us what we know. Mum says something about a lump and its effects, the electricity, the lights that had run down her right side on that morning when she was rushed into hospital – a stroke suspected.

The Glioblastoma

He looks at me. I name it. The glioblastoma. And yet I don't name it: the pain of learning this, the slow realisation that, the need to remind myself – as if these reminders will make it better – that Mum is going to die; I don't name the tears that run down my face when I am alone driving in the car, blaring music, and hearing in my mind my mother call me 'treasure chops' and imagining it being the last time; I don't name the way I imagine my children performing comedy dances and making up poems they're proud of that she won't be able to see or hear; I don't name the night, when we found out, that I stroked my pillow as if I was stroking my infantile baby self and my mother's most vulnerable depths. I just name the type of tumour and hide behind this technical language as if I have some knowledge, which of course in the end I won't. This situation, with its uncertainty and continuous shifting, unfolding, cannot be known. We cannot know if Mum will die peacefully or whether she will fight, and turn and twist in pain till the bitter end. We cannot know.

Dame Tessa Jowell, the ex-Labour minister, died aged seventy with a glioblastoma, having campaigned to improve the diagnosis and treatment options – the range of clinical trials – for people diagnosed with these high-grade cancerous tumours. Having had a brain haemorrhage in May 2018 Jowell remained in a coma until her death that month. Knowing that a woman of repute, high standing, no doubt with the best medical attention, would die within a year of diagnosis brought the reality of Mum's death into focus. Here was a woman of seventy-eight, of ill health generally, and with a sometimes fatalistic attitude – in huge contrast to the determined campaigning of Tessa Jowell.

Writing of her own struggle with GBM, Jessica Morris acknowledges Jowell's commitment to increasing funding, but also notes that the recordings of patient experience and data are often under-analysed, going unnoticed, so that we still know little in subjective terms about the impact of this type of cancer. She notes:

> The 'objective' measures of disease progression, as evidenced by things like the size of my tumour, the results of my MRIs, are prized. The 'subjective' measures of my experience – how I feel each day, my personal responses in terms of X or Y – are largely ignored.
>
> **(*GUARDIAN*, 16 MAY 2018)**

This is because glioblastomas are relatively rare forms of cancer, yet extremely complex owing to the different cell types contained within, and known to be very aggressive: only 5% of those diagnosed will survive five years post-diagnosis. Tessa Jowell died in May, which will in the end be the same month my mother dies in: both women aptly dying in brain tumour awareness month – signified by the colour grey for grey matter. Though I am no campaigner for brain tumours, I hope nonetheless that the lessons stored in my Mum's own unravelling grey matter, the experience that she has shared with us into this debilitating condition can feed into what is already known (and what continues to be unknown) about GBM.

Anticipatory grief

In my work, that part which is dedicated to the education of others, we teach people about the realities of anticipatory grief, once a terminal diagnosis has been made. We see many family members struggle with their reactions to an impending loss.

We know that the period of anticipatory grief can cause different stresses on any family system: roles change, communication may go underground, lives may be put on hold. There can be an understandably heightened concern for the dying person, sometimes with everyone making attempts to get closer to them or to save them from death. I have known families that start to go on as many holidays as they can in the time that they have left, all members signing up to an intense ticking-off of a collective bucket list; or others who put on huge charity events, which satellite around the dying person, a final act of recognition. There are those who re-evaluate the very meaning of their lives, entering into a philosophical or spiritual frame of mind which often focuses on the depth of connection that can be found, which can nonetheless have the effect of creating a sense of isolation or disconnection with relatives who are necessarily functioning on the daily grind of the material plain. Some manage to adapt to the dislocating paradox of living while dying; others complete unfinished business or try to prepare emotionally for what is to come, by talking and sharing fears – sometimes a way of minimising the power of each worrying thought.

None of this preparatory work necessarily means that the absolute loss, through death, of a person we have loved is any easier, despite the weeks or months of anticipation, the chewing over, the imagined absence that might have been available. The finiteness of death is too abstract an idea in the minds of family members awaiting the inevitable. It can also be a reality that is simply too difficult to assimilate and so some will respond by brushing such a truth aside, leaving it to fester in a temporarily sealed part of the unconscious mind. In psychotherapeutic circles we would call this a state of denial, though perhaps this sounds too critical an explanation. We have to ask ourselves what it is that someone is turning away from: and perhaps we find that, while the stakes are high, it is an understandable response, a turning away from the awareness of an intolerable absence yet to come; an anxious holding on out of fear of one's own collapse. As Dr Kathryn Mannix (2018), in her tenderly written book, *With The End in Mind*, writes:

> Using denial to cope with an unbearable sorrow can help someone to avoid facing their distress, but if they can no longer maintain their defence, the cataclysmic truth can rush in like an unstoppable tide, drowning them in their own dread. (p.76)

Coping mechanisms: hope and humour

Clients often tell me that meetings with consultants are filled with anticipation. Hope and expectation find their place next to mounting fear and the possibility of further bad news.

My mother had come to her first appointment with the neurosurgeon in her best coat, eye shadow on beneath her glasses which were attached to a thin cord which hung around her neck. Her language now was almost fully recovered, and despite her usual fatalism, with the 8mg of steroids coursing through her body everything about her spoke of an optimistic woman who was not yet prepared to accept death.

The consultant is joined by the advanced specialist neuro nurse, who had in fact broken the news gently to us during my mother's stay in the hospital while she awaited a more refined MRI as well as an expected biopsy (which, back then, didn't come). The nurse had the most lovely eyes, a gentleness in her face that communicated somehow. Mum seemed to sense this. Eastern European nurse, Greek consultant, and here we are with the government's shambolic Brexit. You can't help but wonder what kind of aggressive tumour is eating away at the heart of our political system...

Before we were shown the scans in the consulting room, I found myself seated attentively with a pad out as if I were taking notes at a keynote speech. It was up to me to capture as much of the conversation as possible: Mum and her brain and Dad with his anxiety, an octogenarian displaced, in a hospital setting which made him ill at ease, upended by the shock, how could it all be taken in? Was I fast becoming the auxiliary mind for the family...? These are the micro-shifts that family members find themselves encountering in the face of terminal illness. There is disruption to the system, like a tapestry with one piece of thread unravelling, the finely tuned interdependencies coming loose and slack. Often the roles re-form, certain tendencies might become more exaggerated or the once-robust member of the system, now ill, fears he will be abandoned as he sees another member take his place. Such changes can create enormous unspoken tension among us all, so entrenched can we become in the expectation others have of us. My father, always the steady and organised one, was so winded by the news that it was becoming more obvious, though not explicit, that I attempt to hold that rational, pragmatic space for us during the meeting. So I sat, listening, with an unfamiliar coolness which somehow protected me from the weight of my feelings.

Language

Sometimes human beings have an uncanny way of masking the troublesome storms below. As Joan Didion (2012) writes, following the shock of her husband's sudden death, she tries to 'straighten out her mind' so much so that the social worker breaking the news to her says of her, 'She's a pretty cool customer.' This phrase remains with her for several pages, such is the disconnect between those inner and outer selves.

The scans, at different angles, showed the location of the tumour, one that wasn't deep, yet resting on top of the centre of the brain responsible for naming objects. In a moment of humour, in the midst of this upheaval, I wondered what an earth we could call this object in Mum's brain, this him or her or ze or xe... memories of *Cat in the Hat*.

It was not till later that afternoon that Mum had named the tumour herself, describing it as the 'silly thing'. 'Funny,' she had said, as she journeyed back to her rural home, 'how it's just a living thing, another thing that wants to go on living. But in its quest to survive, it kills the very source that keeps it growing and thus kills itself. What a silly thing.'

This was one of those moments where you find yourself astonished by someone; how do we find humour in these moments? But we do. Not only had my mother maintained hope in the consultant's room, she had then left his office, briefly taken up rest on a brown leather sofa by the lifts and made a decision about how she would tackle 'the silly living thing' – both her life going forward, how would she live each day, and the bloody tumour itself. Not only did she seem to want to take it all in her stride: on top of that, she seemed to be becoming quite the car seat philosopher.

It is no wonder that the lay person could so easily feel locked out from the medical world, with all its acronyms and specialisms. All professions create boundaries around themselves with language, a club or territory in which those inside are the knowing and those outside the unknowing. Psychotherapeutic theory is not without its linguistic density: countertransference, projection, splitting… Language is a funny thing, which at times brings us closer, yet simultaneously is able to push us further apart. I think about Lacanian psychoanalyst and artist Bracha Ettinger (2006), her quest to discover or to create an ontological language that resists distancing and alienation; her resignification of Lacan's order of the symbolic. What would happen to our relationship, mother and daughter, if common language were gone, would we find a way to hyphenate ourselves back together in some way; find a jointness-in-differentiation (Ettinger, 2006) through other relational means?

Remembering people with dementia, whose semantic memories are out of reach, I had always understood that we can join each other through movement, expression and touch; through all those conscious and unconscious affective flows that exist between subjects. Yet I can be nothing but pained for Mum because, though of course we might find channels of engagement and communication that exist in embodied, intuitive places, it is the spoken word, the written word, the word, the very word – its sounds and curvatures – that resonates for her, that holds her in place, that provides identity, that freed her from the chaos of childhood, and she will miss it beyond measure: for her its loss, we fear, will be an adaptation too far. Language for her has not been a barricade, a way to defend her heart's properties, but rather a way into the heart. And it is not imaginary that this thing in her head has brought her into contact with an even deeper experience of care, as if the recognition of language's limitation and ending is forcing her to use it in love's service. For now at least.

The Biopsy

Mum had decided to get to know 'the silly thing' more intimately. She opted for a biopsy, wanting a more accurate diagnosis of the tumour type. What we already knew was that the glioblastoma was the fastest-growing tumour of the brain. They always start in the brain, rather than having spread from elsewhere in the body. Given the site of Mum's tumour, in the language centre, it seemed ironic that it had a range of nomenclature: grade 4 astrocytoma; glioblastoma multiforme; GBM or GBM4 for short.

Mum decides on a treatment course. The neurosurgeon's biopsy will mean that the glioblastoma will be tested to see if it is responsive to TMZ, a chemotherapy drug temozolomide. It is said that temozolomide works by stopping tumour cells from making new DNA (the material that carries all their genetic information). If the cells cannot make DNA, they cannot divide into new tumour cells, so the tumour cannot grow.

We might imagine that, in lab conditions, a neuropathologist will examine the cells of 'the silly thing', assessing particular patterns of cells. We might imagine that he finds glial cells that have unusual shapes or characteristics – anaplastic glial cells; cells that are dividing rapidly; the appearance of new and extensive blood-transport pathways that are bringing blood to the tumour, allowing it to grow faster... Mum may not want to know all this, some of it sounds like an overcomplicated road network, but we sense she wants to know just what she is dealing with. And how long she might be able to live with it.

Professionals: difficult conversations

That day, on our visit to the neurosurgeon, all three of us had walked into the reception area of the neurosciences outpatient department, Dad twitchy and Mum glad, it seemed, that she had come to get more answers. As we had turned the corner to the seating area, I had seen a familiar face; one of the school mums with whom I had often chatted on the green which stretches out in front of the primary school my children attend. We had looked at one another, surprised, curious why we were both there at the same time. I asked her. She used her head like an arrow, two older people were seated to her right, her mother and father. It was her father.

It stood to reason that her father also had a tumour, something that needed further investigation, dissecting, removing. As my parents and I continued to wait, her family was called first, to see the same neurosurgeon listed on my mother's letter from the hospital. Twenty minutes elapsed, within which time Dad's legs had been jerking up and down, a clear indication that he was already ready to leave. The woman I knew returned to the waiting area, tears in her eyes. 'Glioblastoma,' she had whispered to me, 'found just before Christmas.' Two mothers about to bear witness to the ravages of these aggressive tumours on our parents.

Once she had left, I stared for some time at two wide doors in front of me, with large wooden brown panelling through the centre of the mock pine laminates, unblinking, as if some deity would come to show us the way. It is not uncommon that these brushes with religious or spiritual belief emerge at such times, and we begin to notice not only the desire to be gathered up by something larger than ourselves but also the curious synchronicities found in daily life. Perhaps there is a stripping bare of reason, or a panicked grappling for meaning where none seems forthcoming. Why this other mother, in the reception, on that day? Why, when Mum talks about her childhood in its finest detail, can I now see so clearly the connections with my husband and my children, as if a circle is about to complete itself? Why are certain friends entering my life while others move into the shadows?

I find myself turning to Jung's (1963) writing on life after death:

> ... day after day we live far beyond the bounds of our consciousness, without our knowledge, the life of the unconscious is also going on within us. The more the critical reason dominates, the more impoverished life becomes; but the more of the unconscious, the more of life we integrate. Overvalued reason has this in common with political absolutism: under its dominion the individual is pauperised... Consider synchronistic phenomena, premonitions, and dreams that come true. (p.333)

Perhaps this, in part, is where my mother is at. As her once expert, adept use of language diminishes, with its relationship to order and reason, a more psychic, mystic, unconscious experience flows. I find my mother in different places in her mind, a fresh voice transforming existence with love. One morning, she says:

> 'If you don't block yourself away, and open yourself out to one another, the dimensions of what you can experience are endless... So with this strange thing there has been an intensity of closeness and love, closer than ever before.'

In *A Radical Romance*, Alison Light, writing of the ebbing away of her marriage through Raphael Samuel's terminal cancer, says:

> And time stood still, was concentrated and intensified, sometimes exalted. 'So much sweetness.' I wrote in my diary during the worst of times, by which I meant love. (p. 149)

Each day, I call my parents, asking about the night's sleep, the tablets taken, missing words that may or may not have reappeared. Each day, Mum tells me things are 'fantastic', her reality no doubt a response to the temporary mania of Dexamethasone. Nonetheless this is her new outlook, and, though arguably drug-induced, perhaps there is something of the kind of technicolour view of the world, and its inhabitants, that you might associate with a deeper existential experience. All this enthusiasm for the moment, noticing the way the trees curve around the drive she has driven in and out of for over twenty-seven years; her delight in answering at least four questions on *Eggheads;* the kindness she sees and acknowledges in her husband, my dad, who has brought her cups of tea for the duration of their fifty-seven years together; my husband's quirks, his care; my daughter's mimicry; my son's exact reading; my relatively well-contained concern. She notices it all more than ever before.

This diagnosis, creating juddering disconcerting ripples among us, brings a residual feeling of anticipatory grief to my father and I, the loss of any real certainty in my mother's life, and in their partnership. In the midst of its unbearableness, though, is that inordinate capacity human beings have of seeing their mutual dependencies in the most unexceptional routine moments. Some clients, living alongside spouses with terminal conditions, will come to counselling working and reworking their partnerships in their mind. Over the course of many months, one husband, committed to therapy and to his wife, thought long and hard about what his relationship had meant to him.

His wife has battled cancer for many years now, rounds upon rounds of chemo and radiotherapy, she has endured. Whether it has been the retaining of hope, a gutsy determination or a combination of the right drugs with a relatively kind mutation of cancer, but she has lived a rich life in the face of illness. Globe-trotting, artworks, time with family, she has done it all, but now this woman, who prides herself on her fight and resilience, is weakened by pain and liquid building up ceaselessly in her pleural cavities. He can see the downward spiral though he has seen it before. He fears he may hold the pessimism in the relationship, while his wife takes a momentous stance against decline and death. What is this now, though, her ebbing away or yet another crisis point from which she will bounce back? This time he fears that it can only be the former, her three years prognosis up surely...

They sit on her bed, the pain now too much for simple movement. 'I don't want to die,' she says to him, ensconced in his arms. 'I don't want you to die either,' he says. He talks about the way that, in relation to one another, they have learned how to care and to let go, how to parent, how she has pushed him to take risks, how he has seen her emerge from a once timid skin. He notes the way their lives have coalesced and moved apart, how each one has left an imprint on the other, and how in death that imprint will remain like a permanently etched tattoo on the psychic skin of identity.

In the aftermath of a terminal diagnosis it can be invaluable to find the space to work through the shock and to reflect upon how meaning might be found in such difficult circumstances. A place in which the anger and injustice, and devastating uncertainty, can be encountered and reflected upon with an attuned, robust enough other can be vital. It can allow partners and family members to think about tricky conversations that might need expression, to explore regrets of times past or the possible regrets of things left unspoken. To be recognised in our pain somehow allows us to bear it, just that little bit more.

LIVING WITH
UNCERTAINTY

'Look on each day as if it were your last, and each
unlooked for hour will seem a boon.'

Horace, *Epistles. 15 BC*

The language of uncertainty is used often in a palliative
care context, particularly in relation to the experience
of living with a terminal disease. Though someone
with a life-limiting condition can be presented with the
option of treatment plans, with a view either to cure, to slow
down or to control symptoms, the anxiety that living with
impending loss brings cannot be underestimated. Treatment
possibilities for many terminally ill people represent a
symbol of hope, or heroics, and an imagined future, albeit
one punctuated by hospital appointments and sometimes
gruelling interventions. There are of course many patients
who are given fewer treatment options, or where, at some
point, a treatment possibility will be withdrawn: a tumour
may be pressing down on a main artery, for example, or the

patient is already in too fragile a physical state to endure another round of drugs.

For my mother, owing to her poor health and an existing atrial fibrillation, the reality was that a resection of the GBM tumour was simply too risky. Following a biopsy there was a possibility of chemo drugs to slow the disease progression, but ultimately we knew that she was likely to die within a year. Of course this kind of news can lead people to a sense of despair, and the wish to give up. What can we celebrate when we are so definite about time being up?

Reflecting space

With the reality of such precariousness, then, how does a person continue to live each day without succumbing to an all-encompassing, heavy experience of anticipatory grief? Finding a space in which to talk about current losses, as well as fears of further future dispossessions, can allow a person to tap into those parts of identity that he or she might hide from family members. If we are intent on maintaining the façade of strength in the face of uncertainty this can sometimes lead us to a sense of isolation and exclusion.

A partner, too, may also feel shut out, and rejected, which can at times result in tense, fraying relationships. I have known couples test one another, a competition developing around whose needs are highest – for instance, the terminally ill husband who still looks well or the wife, juggling childcare, work and a home life, buckling under the pressure. Finding balance can be terribly difficult, particularly if an illness is seen to support an already asymmetrical way of relating, a husband or wife in such circumstances can be overly critical, punitive almost of the partner living with a disease that will one day end a life. Honest and open discussion may well provide a chance to explore not only the conflicts involved in day-to-day living but also a history of unspoken resentments that might play out more intensely at this time. Beyond this, and more hopefully, embarking on psychotherapy together will also offer couples an opportunity to reassess where pleasure can be found in both joint and individual experience, as the changes of a particular condition mount up. For some this might also offer scope for reflection about those relational dynamics that predate any illness and which could possibly mirror – for both parties – an unease around being a caregiver or a recipient of care, possibly stemming from internalised childhood patterns with parental figures.

Psychotherapy and counselling in palliative care can have a very important place. The therapeutic relationship in the lives of clients with life-limiting conditions makes for a safe and facilitating environment in which the messier, untidy truths of the experience can be talked about: a place to download those days of struggle and tiredness and tension, which people fear are burdensome for family and friends. A therapist, then, must be open to noticing and to attending to both the moments of continued joy in someone's life – where it can be found and how it can be maintained – as well as the experiences in which a client and their family worries they are coming undone. The work is not about creating false hope and reassurance, but rather sitting with the paradox of pain and panic alongside the reports, which can be surprising to hear, of continued value in the present moments of the everyday as well as plans – occasionally very exciting ones – for the future.

It was of course strange for me, on occasion, to take up this role in my mother's life, and simultaneously a great privilege to do so. Like many of my clients, Mum also needed to talk at length about the significant points in her life, some of which she repeated over and over again. These spoken acts were akin to what Crociani-Windland (2013) talks about when she says, 'We go back and we repeat, in order to go forward.' (p. 348) In my mother's case, it seemed that the going forward was into a place she could knit together experiences and associations – moments overlapping, unravelling and rewound through different understandings and perspectives – in order to shed some sort of skin which would allow for a more accepting death. My mother had in fact been a knitter: a knitter is someone who can sit still for hours at a time, undoing and redoing until a piece is complete. It was as if she were doing this in conjunction with me, as many of my clients do, creating some sort of blanket of her life. It seems in some ways poignant, since the word *palliative* itself is originally from the Latin *pallium*, which means to cloak: a cloak of comfort and care through the psychic, social, spiritual and physical pain of the dying soul.

Yet applying this metaphor to therapeutic work with the dying is a little idealised, too neat and tidy: sometimes people die with loose threads left behind for family, leaving them bewildered, confused and saddened. Alison Light (2019) notes that death is not necessarily a summing up, but quite simply 'a fact'. Sometimes death can be a very messy fact.

There are times in therapy when clients seek answers to questions that they feel unable to ask; it is not uncommon for people to fear the risk of unsettling the comfort of the status quo. In death, this can come at a high price.

> She keeps on replaying the moment that he tells her that her sister is his soulmate, and that he has exhausted himself caring for her. Her marriage feels wrecked, she fears he has never loved her. Yet then she says she keeps

finding notes, scrawled in bright colours, that he has left her in her favourite photography books, or stapled to the calendar expressing only love and gratitude for their fifty year-long marriage. Was it the drugs that made him cruel before he died? Was his brain addled from a lack of oxygen? Why did he spare the children from his anger? Or was their 'good marriage' also embedded in ambivalences and fantasies of other possible mates; ambivalences which arguably exist in all loving relationships but which tend to go underground? What were these loose ends that plagued her in her bereavement? Was there more hate than love? And now he is gone, and she never asked him.

Psychotherapy will not have the answers to these conundrums that can eat away at the bereaved, but being able to relinquish some of the shame and humiliation of existing in a relationship that was not ever fully known – or enduring a marriage with someone who seemed to have changed into someone unrecognisable – without sensing a judgement can be invaluable. Often, this gives the client – not initially of course – the chance to recognise his or her contributions to the way a relationship has formed and proceeded. It is in this process that we may see a new blanket emerge that is able to envelop someone into the future, with less guilt perhaps but with a greater depth of learning; the possibility of a new script based on new awarenesses. Just sometimes…

Of course, I continued to be my mother's daughter until her very last words. Even in her increasing decline she continued to chastise me for eating too many nuts in case they damaged my teeth, or failing to brush my hair, a hangover from her once narcissistic maternal stance. But I was also a friend who listened, finding threads of meaning in the fragments that she recalled. For my mother, as her language use broke down, these fragments became all the more important, as if they were a way in to understanding the whole of her without narrative flow. As Joe Wood (2019) writes in the *Polyphony*:

> [G]ood end-of-life care, which is so much about the whole person whose life-story is coming to an end, might also be based as much on a single utterance that reduces an individual's experience to a few synonymous words but, in leaving the rest silent, allows their experience to be communicated more universally.

Sometimes, despite her increasingly shaky and potted version of events, we were able to rework the guilt and shame that she carried with her about being too disciplinary as a teacher or a mother. We tried to reframe these difficult feelings in the context of her long life and a childhood without bounds. And I wondered then, as I do now, whether there was something about this unburdening that helped her to continue to live, with relative lightness, as the tumour gradually reassembled, or disassembled, her sense of self. Stolorow (2011) writes, drawing on a Heideggerian frame of reference, of moving into a sense of greater authenticity (a liberation from the gaze of the 'they-self' of Dasein) when a person makes an emotional shift from being preoccupied by shame into residing more comfortably in existential guilt and grief. He writes:

> In shame, we are held hostage by the eyes of others; we belong, not to ourselves, but to them... Such a shift toward what really matters to one as an individual must not be equated with narcissistic self-absorption and self-centeredness. What really matters can be one's love and

caring for another or others. In authentic existing, we must own up, not only to our own finitude, but also to the finitude of all those whom we love and to whom we are deeply connected. (p. 286)

Strikingly, and always surprisingly, the mainstay of Mum's fragments seemed to oscillate between an ontological message of 'Love, love, love' – akin to Stolorow's (2010) notion of authenticity – and a much more mundane preoccupation with blue, or red, or brown food. The contradictoriness, and nuance, of dying people's fragments is captured beautifully in palliative care doctor Nathan Gray's (2019) series of cartoons about the privilege of being alongside the terminally ill. His comics depict the meaningful wonder, the reflection, the gratitude and love, the summing up of life, as well as the monotony of wanting one's own bed, or drinking milk again, and the mess and grudges that continue.

Living with fragmentation, and the multiple characteristics of these fragments, better describes my mother's life in those months before she died. For my father, though, whose sense of self continued to feel relatively coherent, he assured me, it was the continual anxiety of living with uncertainty that best captured the quality of his daily life. While he still held on to his routines, his beliefs and values, he began to notice that the relative structure of routine that provided some stability was nonetheless punctured by some thought or another of what would become or unbecome, destabilising him for several minutes at a time.

Routines and new routines: consistency and adaptation

Over the last two weeks my parents have established a new routine. They wake, within minutes of one another, at around 3am each morning. Mum has moved into what has up till now been my father's study, where he has watched, in solitary confinement, French political discussions; where he has typed letters furiously to the *Guardian* about the state of the education system, a neoliberal agenda that swallows up human minds greedily and spits out even greedier consumers; where he produces short-form poetry about what he sees outside his window in the dewy mornings. Mum has moved into this space, and Dad seems to need so much less of his own now. The physical closeness between them speaks possibly of the anxiety of impending separation, and of course also two lives whose stories have run alongside and through each other.

Mum is sleeping in this cosy room. Once we realised that Mum would no longer manage the stairs, a bed that my children used was brought down from upstairs. Upstairs, downstairs, my father now sleeping on the wide, king-size bed that was once theirs; Mum in the single bed by his desk. At 3am they meet, my father checking in on his wife, 'his gem', and together they have a cup of hot chocolate and a biscuit. They talk. Sometimes Mum recounts episodes of her life that my father is surprised to learn either because he has forgotten or she has never told him. Recently she opened up about a former French boyfriend, who had written to her a week into her marriage with my father, suggesting that they meet in Wales. It was too late. By then Mum had a ring on her finger, and had taken up residence in a caravan on the tops of the cliffs in Pennard, the Gower.

In the quiet stillness of night, this ritual takes place and there is a sweetness to it. Closer than ever; a cramped – yet cosy – space replicating that first home in the caravan perhaps. I wonder how my dad will be when these comforting night-time meetings are over: will he move into that one room in the cottage? Despite his historic quest for solitude and introversion, the impending loneliness must frighten him, for till now being alone in the context of a long, enduring marriage has been his choice, because his isolation is always in relation to the presence – the always-thereness – of my mother. Soon there will be no choice. I think of the many models of grief we psychotherapists have at our disposal (see chapter 4, Freud, 1917; Kubler-Ross, 1969; Worden, 1991; Stroebe & Schutt, 1995/6; Klass, 1996) and wonder where Dad will find himself among these carefully conceptualised theories. Will he be frightened that a grieving experience is so far outside the 'normal attitude to life' (Freud, 1917) that he has had, that he may lurch from moments where he is imprisoned in the small details of each memory to a more frightening desire to obliterate all forms of the past, and even images of Mum? Will his grief take him to places where he sees first-hand how papery and slippery sanity can be? Many clients who have endured long marriages find themselves tormented by the silence that absence brings; many put on the radio all day and night long, if only to fill space; others distract themselves endlessly with groups and trips, such is the shock of being plunged into a state of aloneness (Winnicott, 1958), a state which arouses deep anxiety in some.

He says that he was becoming exhausted as her dementia took hold; and she was waking through the night. The cancer he could manage but having to translate her garbled expressions in the early hours was more than he could bear. He found himself becoming ill, and feels a failure for asking for help. At least he kept it in the family.

He stares at her photograph now on top of the fireplace, one where they are dancing and laughing together. He has to turn away from it. Sometimes he is tempted to turn the photograph itself to the wall. He listens to audio books each day, the longer the better, so that at least there is someone talking in his home, to fill the silence and to drown out the guilty noise in his head. As he talks about keeping busy – going for long walks, getting some pets, joining a choir, seeing his children, booking holidays – there is the crack, the first of his tears, 'I just miss her,' he says, 'anything for a few minutes of her time.'

For children that grieve a parent, our world also becomes dislodged, the structure that held us dismantled, but those of us who have reached adulthood may well be lucky enough to have reached an age where we have our own family, our own dependents and responsibilities. For those who lost their parents as children, the grief will no doubt become part of their ongoing identity. As Porter (2015) narrates on behalf of the boys, an acknowledged autobiographical device, whose mother died during their childhood:

We seem to take it in ten-year turns to be defined by it, sizeable chunks of cracking on, then great sink-holes of melancholy.

Same as anyone, really. (p. 96)

And so while a chain of reactions, of going over mnemic ground, might ensue we still get up and plough on with duties, with concerns that keep us rooted to the structure of our adult lives. Not all, of course; for some people relationships have an adhesive quality, where grown children have never forged a path all that separate to their parents: in cases like these the grief may manifest a sense of being stuck, the fear that in any moment's forgetting some well-masked ambivalence may find its way to the surface.

For me, though, close ties had over time loosened, a paradox of further separation brought about the mutual recognition – the fullness of existing subjectivities in all guises – that Benjamin (2006) so eloquently talks about.

Small or forbidden pleasures

As a child I used to call my parents the cuckoo clock people, and it seems ironic that a curious internalised cuckoo chimes each morning at 3am for my parents, both popping up, awake, to sit and to share. It is clear that one way that my parents are living with the uncertainty evoked by Mum's terminal diagnosis is by creating new routines, finding ways to enjoy small pleasures that can so easily be overlooked when we exist, as some of us do, at high speed. And so they have a cup of tea, and eat some thin, refined cappuccino biscuits. Though I am glad that they are tucking in, a niggling concern is simultaneously eating away at me.

Having scoured the internet, I have discovered that, according to some authorities, the ingestion of sugar is a treat for cancer. Cancer, it seems, feeds off glucose and fructose found not only in biscuits and cakes, but in carbohydrates too. What is this niggle, though? An expression of ambivalence towards the maternal figure… a desire to tell her what she should do in the same way that she had tried to force feed me when I was small, her tongue protruding from her lips, representative of her own desire to be fed; was I about to use the biscuits against her, to control her, a final, coercive role reversal? It was unlikely, I said to myself, surely such resentments had been put to bed in my twenties. Yet ambivalences, of course, in relationships are never far from the surface in the domain of the living and the dying. Adam Phillips (2015), essayist and British psychotherapist, makes this statement forcefully:

> In Freud's vision of things we are, above all, ambivalent animals: wherever we hate, we love; wherever we love, we hate. If someone can satisfy us, they can also frustrate us; and if someone can frustrate us, we always believe that they can satisfy us. We criticize when we are frustrated — or when we are trying to describe our frustration, however obliquely — and praise when we are more satisfied, and vice versa. Ambivalence does not, in the Freudian story, mean mixed feelings, it means opposing feelings… these contradictory feelings are our 'common source' ; they enter into everything we do. They are the medium in which we do everything. We are ambivalent, in Freud's view, about anything and everything that matters to us; indeed, ambivalence is the way we recognize that someone or something has become significant to us… Where there is devotion there is always protest… (p. 85)

Psychotherapists in palliative care are no less exposed to the opposing feelings of their clients towards spouses and parents, and other family members, than practitioners working in other sessions. The only perceivable difference is that we are often working with the explicit awareness of the ticking clock, so often there is a sense of urgency involved in providing time, space and thought to people to disentangle the feelings in order to support relationships undergoing not only change but termination. The following vignette is an example of supporting couples emotionally at such a time:

Caring for him at home is becoming increasingly difficult, a marital dynamic that has always filled with tension. Now his brain tumour makes him ever more anxious, confused and demanding whenever she leaves the room. For her, there is no let up. This need of his, a fear of loss has plagued him since a boy, whose parents perished early on, and he controls her; sometimes he rejects her, sometimes he pulls her closer. In turn, she seeks distance from his oppressiveness, yet seeks him out when he is cold. This push and pull is pronounced; it is live in the room. We go over his experience as a young abandoned boy – the nameless dread now stirred up in the face of his wife's absence, his only anchor at this most bewildering time. We talk about her youth, too, and the way she took flight from demanding parents, escaping the family home as soon as she could. Together they begin to see a pattern to their lives, to their inversely correlated proximity and distant-seeking behaviours but sadly there is very little time to make it good.

Here I am now, thankful for the career I have chosen, the training, the understanding through it that I developed about my mother's fear of separation, of her inflexible moral codes, her need to control the path she believed should be mine. Relatedly, I am glad that I have also been gifted with time to get to know her as a flawed, clay-footed parent, at the same time through this lens of experiential knowledge. In adolescence many of us have to stand apart forcefully in order to explore ourselves; we have to push against the real and internalised patriarchs and matriarchs to affirm and reaffirm ourselves. Faced with the relatively long life of a parent, this is all well and good, for there is time to relate in fresh ways, through new understandings. For adolescents who lose their parents as they are on the cusp of this developmental push, the guilt of the fantasised rejection of their parents, or indeed more murderous inclinations towards a mum or dad, lingers and debilitates; the guilt for adolescents that we sometimes come across in palliative care is stifling and oppressive. For many the anger and hostility that needed to be directed outwards towards authority figures goes inwards and underground, manifesting itself in self-harming behaviours – cutting and alcoholism – and suicidal ideation. Grief can of course be very complex indeed, with therapists taking on maternal or paternal roles in the countertransference as love is perhaps reworked and rediscovered, where projections are finally taken back in so that the continuation of life is possible.

As a woman in her middle years, however, those struggles for me, those tensions, were long gone. So now I see in my mother both her care for me, and also her vulnerability. I want to be able to give back as much as I can.

Alain de Botton (2017) writes in *The Course of Love*:

> We start off in childhood, believing parents might have access to a superior kind of knowledge and experience. They look for a while astonishingly competent. Our exaggerated esteem is touching and also intensely

problematic, for it sets them up as the ultimate objects of blame when we gradually discover that we are flawed, sometimes unkind, in areas ignorant and utterly unable to save us from certain troubles. It can take a while, until the fourth decade or the final hospital scenes, for a more forgiving stance to emerge. Their new condition, frail and frightened, reveals in a compellingly physical way something which has always been true psychologically: that they are uncertain vulnerable creatures motivated more by anxiety, fear, a clumsy love and unconscious compulsions than by godlike wisdom and moral clarity – and cannot, therefore, forever be held responsible for either their own shortcomings or our many disappointments. (p. 205)

I reflect on how glad I am that I haven't waited till now to be able to recognise my mother in all her paradoxes. Yet this thin sugary coffee-flavoured biscuit that she eats at 3am niggles still. With the raft of information about Ketogenic diets, their capacity to slow down the growth of cancerous tumours with protein-rich and low-sugar foods, I find myself wanting to tell my mother to minimise carbs, to throw the biscuits and the fudge yoghurt out… I realise that I would, in fact, clutch at any straws – however magical – to make her live. Beyond being a mother, she is my friend. We have known one another for over forty-four years now; we have experienced and discussed each other's flaws, laughed at them even; a once fraught relationship, the jostling of identities, transformed many years ago into something altogether lighter. She is in fact the easiest person to go on holiday with.

Several years ago, I invited her to Northumberland with our children. A large woman in size, she squeezed into a tiny, fourteen-year-old Micra gifted to us by my dead father-in-law:

it rattled all the way from the South of England into the darkness of night to the castle-town of Warkworth, where we struggled to find the small terraced house we had booked for our stay. Mum had laughed and laughed – in fact her laugh is more representative of her than her signature – and so we repeated a few more holidays with the children around the British Isles, because for all of us there was a genuine easy contentment in the journeying and in the comedy of our clumsy adventures.

But back to this biscuit, with its crispy bite: I realise that it is imbued with conflicting meaning. I see it as a gift in some ways – part of this wonderful newly emerging quality of life that Mum has with my father at 3am – and a curse, the strange, possibly deadly, pleasure that may or may not make those glioblastoma cells grow even faster than they might be doing already.

When I read an article, quoting the CEO of Cancer Council Australia, Professor Sanchia Aranda, I feel relief. 'Stopping sugar getting to cancer cells would also mean that your body's healthy cells get starved of necessary sugars… I think that would make you lose weight, [and] would make your immune system less efficient and more likely that a cancer would progress.'

Like all illnesses, whether they be physical or psychological, there are reams of confusing and contradictory information. It is easy to get lost. It reminds me of the leaflets, the bundles that health visitors provide, the endless pages the internet peddles, for fledgling mothers gathering up their newborns in those first few weeks. Information to some extent, as the mantra goes, is knowledge, is power. But sometimes it puts you at such a distance from your instinct, from an embodied knowledge, within the grooves of human experience. I hold on to the thought that for my mother, right now, these small choices about her own intake are what keep her going. And so the biscuit at 3am must go on. It is one of her little, yet essential, joys.

When someone is dying it can be tempting to try to keep him or her alive: in creating strict regimes, offering up nutritional advice, early morning meditation – whatever it is – we think we might have their best intentions at heart. Sometimes we might want to keep feeding someone who is slowly losing the will and inclination to take in food – the body is shutting down; it can be so hard to let go in this way. Food for many cultures is a symbol of nurturing and so we might feel that we have to nourish the dying person, or indeed only give them healthy options.

Total pains

Yet, working in end-of-life care, as I do, my understanding of care has gradually been reshaped. Following the ground-breaking nurse and founder of the first modern hospice, St Christopher's, Dame Cicely Saunders, those of us in palliative care are working with some conceptualisation of total pain in mind. Cicely Saunders, who would have been 100 years old in June 2019, understood that simply having someone to talk to could be a major relief. Of course, this is one of the reasons why counselling and psychological support is embedded in palliative care. The recognition of the value of talking and listening strikes at the heart of the notion of total pain. What Saunders (1967) pushed for was a focus on the whole person, a focus she felt was missing in hospice care during the 1960s and '70s. Countering a medicalised approach to death and dying, she acknowledged that the pain of a dying person was not simply located in the physical body, but had made in-roads into the social, psychological and spiritual aspects of individual identity. Pain may emerge in relation to difficult family dynamics exploding around the dying person, or in a client's emerging anger towards his or her faith, a sense of being abandoned by an unreliable God.

In other words, Saunders was interested in pain as a way into understanding individual identity, perhaps offering someone the freedom of being known, validated, appreciated before it is too late. If the particularity of human pain could be seen, heard and responded to we might imagine that Saunders' logic was that some peace could eventually be found in the dying process. As a result, the practice of palliative care, centred as it is around this core concept of total pain, draws on the expertise of a variety of professionals working within different disciplines, some working pragmatically to fulfil important fundamental needs and others within the domain of meaning-making and spirituality, yet coming together to hold in mind the multiple needs of the person in their care in order to alleviate suffering, 'physical, psychosocial and spiritual' (World Health Organisation, 2002). The pain must be thought about holistically, through the effort of multiple professionals, thus becoming everybody's business (National Palliative and End of Life Care Partnership, 2015). While it is of course important to offer clients psychotherapy or chaplaincy to rescript or visit existential and spiritual dilemmas, we also know that distress has social components; a patient fearing that her family will become impoverished or destitute when she is no longer a salaried employee will experience heightened anxiety and pain until her circumstances are improved. Interiority, while being the bread and butter work, the prime interest of the psychotherapist, is always embedded in that wider net of discursive practices and social reality, which for some is filled with struggle, benefits, poor housing and deprivation.

Of course, the ideals of theory and policy do not always play out in the lived experience of the dying: we know that there is an inequity of provision for older people, particularly those with dementia, people from ethnic minorities and those from the LGBT community, as well as homeless people and those in prisons (Dixon et al, 2015). There are of course barriers and facilitators which hinder, or which may close the policy-practice gap. The facilitating picture is a complex one but improved education and counselling for staff, as well as better funding and the resourcing of palliative care (all too often reliant on individual fundraising schemes, such as the shaving of heads, cup-cake sales and treks to Machu Picchu!), make a real difference to provision and holistic care. We hear regularly from those advocating for reforms in palliative care, bemoaning the lack of financial support from the national government. Tracey Bleakley, CEO of Hospice UK, has a pinned tweet on her Twitter account, asking:

> Should access to hospice care (complex end-of-life healthcare) covered by the NHS constitution, under NICE guidelines, regulated by CQC be dependent on how many second hand clothes can be sold & marathons sponsored in the local area? Is this the society we want?

It is the question that most of us in the field of care are asking. What does this absence of investment in palliative, health and social care signify? As with dementia care, palliative care represents that final undoing, a period of intense high dependency – akin to the absolute attentive care that may be forthcoming for a newborn entering the bewildering flashing lights of the world. But the dying person is moving out of the world, the reverse trajectory, and into either nothingness or into the cosmos, to a new body reincarnated, depending on our cultural beliefs. So why might it be so hard for us societally and politically to support this ultimate process of dependency, of letting go, with the respect and investment any human life so deserves?

So I come full circle back to this idea of total pain, and my mother's early-morning biscuit. For her this was becoming a social moment with my father, for him a companionship he cherished; a point at which their emotional worlds rediscovered each other, a living Venn diagram of overlapping needs. We might imagine that this biscuit, which may have expedited the growth of Mum's already aggressive tumour, was nonetheless a way in to ensuring that her emotional and social pains – the fear of holding things in or experiencing her demise in isolation – were minimised. With this understanding, a psychic one over a medicalised one, I bought them both several more boxes of these slender Italian delicacies to enjoy.

To live with the uncertainty of dying, and its unfolding, may become a little more bearable if some of the uncertainties can be shared with close others; when our vulnerabilities, memories, fears for the future – all those powerful imaginings, thoughts and feelings that will invariably be evoked – can be talked about somehow. It seemed that Mum and Dad had found a way to do just that. As Lisa Appignanesi writes in her beautiful and candid account of grief, *Everyday Madness: On Grief, Anger and Love,* 'No life can be lived without support' (p9). And that, we might imagine, takes us right to the very very end.

The agency of the dying person

In dementia care (Ramsay-Jones, 2019), we talk about the slow, gradual loss of a person we once knew; how they change in front of us from being speaking adults to those who mutter or make sounds; from having roles as grandparents or parents to returning to the re-imagined roles they may have had as young adults, in work or otherwise; from being fully cognisant one moment, to clutching on to names and faces that evaporate the next. Sometimes, in all of this muddle, we can discover a mutuality based on new recognitions, roles and languages, if of course there is an openness to such explorations in those of us who are well. It seems that, for my father and I, we might be entering into a similar dimension with Mum and her glioblastoma.

There are some parallels between the experience of dementia, and of malignant brain cancer – both of which have found their way, at different times, into our family – since the changes taking place neurologically have an impact on cognition, memory, language, spatial awareness, behaviour, bodily movement. Some talk about those with dementia or with a glioblastoma as being no longer recognisable (Dartington, 2010), having lost their sense of self or their former identities. But perhaps the inability to recognise people who are changing and shifting and moving into different states is about us, about the ways in which we categorise and force each other into inflexible places, limited by our own narrow capacity to discern the very deepest sentient experience of what it is to be human.

It is said, for instance, that the limbic brain, which carries our emotions – fear and love – emerged in the first mammals. In these conditions, where arguably there is a trajectory towards unbecoming, where the brain is not performing as expected, we might find in someone a return to a pre-verbal, pre-conscious strata of existence where that person feels more than he thinks; where the immediacy of the moment is more valued than the anticipation of future plans; where connection with attuned others holds the greatest value. Quite possibly, in this bewildering journey of dispossession, of the loss of the 'rational' mind, there is in turn nonetheless a repossession of a fundamental humane time-space where in fact we feel and touch our way through each day. Perhaps if we were able to attend slowly to the micro-interactions of someone with dementia or with a malignant brain tumour as it advances, for instance, which can of course be hard work, there might be a lesson there for all of us... and a rediscovery of our affective access to the other, from which perhaps we have long since distanced ourselves, sometimes through the conditioning function of parental and societal norms. If we look behind our own emotional armour, behind the trappings of success and the accessories of ego, we might just start to recognise those whose cognitive abilities evade them, as someone not all that dissimilar from ourselves. From here it might be possible to see what it is to engage in intimacies and tendernesses beyond speech, beyond cognition, that we never quite thought possible − and to finally reimagine our responsibility towards one another throughout the life course.

Before my mother was diagnosed with a GBM multiforme, I had seen similar changes take place in clients. For therapists who work with, and family carers who look after, those who are dying with brain cancer or dementia, or with any condition that gradually erodes factual and semantic memory and motor function, affects behaviours and disinhibits, sitting with the helplessness and anxiety of a client can be incredibly painful. Nonetheless, bearing witness to such pain, this awful debilitating fragmentation, can at times provide a client with a sense of solidity that usually feels out of reach, a momentary regaining of calm when all is at sea. Therapy can help to provide a containment of mind and security for someone, a place to share primal anxiety and raw undigested feeling. While the function of the brain will not be repaired, therapy − the consistency of visit, time and the trusting relationship that develops − for people living with cognitive losses can offer some emotional scaffolding that may contain the fears of falling apart. As the client slows down cognitively the therapist too must mirror this pace and attune more to embodied micro-movements; home visits might become frequent. While it can be a challenge to keep the physical frame, the internal frame of meaning-making that therapists may draw on can come into its own, as clients invite us into the private spaces in their home paralleling those very private spaces in their minds. I have been reminded time and time again of work and research I have done in dementia care homes (Ramsay-Jones, 2019) when encountering clients in the community with Parkinson's, MS, brain cancer who have started to experience erratic neural signalling and hence cognitive impairments, as follows:

> She shows her daughter the teabags and cries, two joined together. 'What shall I do? These first or the kettle? What do I do with them? Tear them in two? I can't remember. A cup, we need them. I have done the…' She stumbles verbally, and points to a silver teapot. 'Shall we have it in that thing?' She scratches her skull and then the sides of her cheeks, she performs this motion with some force as if she is urging her mind to work again. She carries on scratching, her daughter strokes her back as if to offer some calm through touch. Her mother lets out a sigh, as if her daughter's care is giving her permission to unburden herself. 'It's all going,' she says. The simplest of words; the simplest of tasks. All going.

Over the last two days each time I hear Mum on the telephone I notice that her words are getting lost or twisted; socks, shoes, easy objects become thingamabobs; 'maths' gets muddled with 'football'; some words are on the tip of her tongue, sounding breathless; great determination is needed to push them from that soggy area of her brain beyond to her listeners. The signal is bad, static breaking down the line between her and me.

Mum does not, I fear, want to talk as long anymore. Those giggly, chatty days are slipping away. Only an uptake of steroids will bring them back, but she resists a doubling of doses. She does what she is told when it comes to doctors and the prescribed dosage of pills. What we learn from the neuro-oncology nurse is that higher doses of steroids can lead to muscle waste. The plan long term is to reduce them incrementally, although this is likely to dismantle the structures of language even further. Right now, at least, Mum is still keen to tell me about one or two of her daily adventures. Tomorrow she is off to find grey and deep red duvets because she wants to look the part – theatrical, stage curtains spring to mind, we might imagine – in the hospital bed the district nurse has recently had delivered to the cottage. This is so that Mum can control the ups and downs of her swelling legs; an issue, genetic, that she shares with her two sisters. Mum is delighted, as is my father, that this kind of speedy, efficient care is available. She feels well looked after and, most importantly, listened to.

Advance care planning

Research (Haun et al, 2014) shows that with early intervention from palliative care agencies, and supporting teams, a person with incurable advanced cancer has the chance of a better quality of life. This may also extend survival times. As well as having a new hospital bed in situ, Mum is also relieved to write up an advance care plan with the help of an American palliative care nurse, who visited very soon after her diagnosis and whom she warmed to, partially because of his love of the dramatic arts and a fervent anti-Trump sentiment. Advance care planning or anticipatory care planning, as it is called in Scotland, is used to plan out someone's end of life care. The process involves some reflection about the wishes and needs that a dying person may have as they near the end of their lives. People might have preferences about where they may wish to be cared for, a desired place of death, the treatments that they wish to avoid. Planning such as this can happen at any time, possibly needing to be revised at different stages.

The goal, and thinking behind advance care planning, is to make sure that someone's wishes are heard, noted and acted upon, and that relevant care is coordinated in tandem with these wishes. Advance directives can also be included, where treatments can be refused such as CPR, considered to be a brutally invasive intervention for those with a terminal illness. The advance care planning process will also involve discussions around the need for lasting powers of attorney, particularly for those who are likely to undergo cognitive decline. The Gold Standards Framework (2018) says that the advance care planning process should involve thinking; talking between family members; recording wishes and needs; discussing them with health professionals, including discussions about resuscitation; and finally sharing them with all those who need to know within the system of care.

Advocates of advance care planning, as per the charity Compassion in Dying whose sister organisation is Dignity in Dying, promote the idea that completing advance care plans and directives means that end-of-life decisions are a person's own; that quality of life will be better if such wishes are known. For my mother, there was some truth in this, and we all sensed her relief that she was able to make her voice heard, her choices known. For Mum it seemed to make this ultimately uncontrollable, messy situation more orderly, a set of ground rules for dying. In the midst of such precariousness, this draw towards the predictable, or at least the fantasy of predictability, could be understood. While advance care planning was undoubtedly of use to her, a woman whose childhood was often characterised by chaos and unpredictability, the idea of a plan seemed to hold her together. While death cannot be avoided, on a more abstract level, it does seem that this kind of intervention – of phantasied neatness and planning – is perhaps also a societal response to anything uncontained, uncontrollable, irrational experiences that the dying – as well as many, many others – have to face. Such professionalism arguably helped to contain the workers too, faced as we are with the trickier, uglier aspects of the dying process. All of this perhaps feeds into a medicalised definition of death as a technical problem which has to be predictable, managed and controlled (Seymour, 1999).

Though my mother would not have had it any other way, I couldn't help wondering about the way that dying patients were being set up as self-regulating service users – while also buying into this notion, owing to the real, yet sometimes overstated, rewards of autonomous functioning – and that in some ways such plans could also be used in the judgement of services, underpinning and providing further momentum for a widespread surveillance culture in health and social care. I imagined an MDT (multi-disciplinary team) meeting following Mum's death: did Joyce Margaret Jones get her preferred place of death, or did we let her down?

And I was back, it seemed, in the loop of my mind at least, to this societal preoccupation with getting these painful – yet natural – human experiences *right* for people, and this concept of 'right' always seemed implicitly linked to the amount of choice a person has. The experience of dying, like life itself, is full of moments of not-knowing, and yet in current policy and practice it seems so very hard to make room for the fear of not-knowing and for that which cannot be controlled; the desire to make certain the uncertain makes those decisive pathways turn into something altogether more perplexing. It tends to err on the side of managing us all, of quashing our fears, boiling down the inarticulable into tick boxes. Sometimes the sheer weight of thinking about death in the patient and for their family makes daily life unimaginable: patients may threaten to kill themselves or may begin to drink excess alcohol, or liquid morphine, to numb the psychic pain – these situations cannot be managed or controlled, and may need an altogether different approach.

He has been putting a fruity vodka-mix down his feeding tube, and his family feel they have lost him to a raging spirit that inhabits him in his dying days. His wife is frightened of his outbursts, not knowing when he will become volcanic; and what she might say to provoke it. She fears she is becoming the abandoning mother of his childhood. He leaves crazed and crazy messages on her phone, and everyone is walking on eggshells. She worries that he doesn't see her anymore but some strange projected phantasmagorical hallucination. Who is she in relation to him? How is she being used? One day, he manages to express himself, tells her he is like Munch's The Scream. Dying has awoken all those repressed primordial fears of falling apart, and not being gathered by a robust enough maternal object, fears that he has prettified, edited his whole adult life; and now he succumbs to his once so tightly controlled unconscious. One image giving way to another.

So while the plans that Mum had made arguably gave her a felt-sense of control, I wondered whether beneath the surface she was denying us the opportunity of hearing any other realities. She never said.

Family systems: to tell or not to tell

Nonetheless, with her advance care plan in place and her shifting routines with my father, Mum seemed to be in a contented place, accepting of her predicament with stoicism.

She tells me about her visits to her own ageing sister, who has been living in a nursing home since the death of her own husband. My aunty, Mum's sister, is cognitively able but physically her body is breaking down. She has developed drop foot and can no longer visit the shops that she once loved to walk about. Mum has not told my aunty about her brain cancer, nor her other sister who lives in the Deep South of America.

I imagine the missed opportunities that sharing this news may bring about. What would they all say to one another if only they knew? Would new ways of relating and sociability be discovered, would past lives and family history of silencing death finally be lifted? It is not uncommon for people to keep bad news from their family members, telling only the closest people to them. Sometimes we want to continue for as long as possible to maintain the roles we have always had in a family system, perhaps a protective measure to avoid being reminded of the fate you will soon meet. Mum was establishing a clearly demarcated boundary around those who knew and those who wouldn't, those circles of inner and outer trust. Would my small family and my father allow her to hold on to her dominion? Would her sisters try to take over as older sisters do?

Professionals working in palliative care may find themselves at times acting as managers to a boundary between the patient and the family beyond. Sometimes we mediate, prompting the difficult questions and conversations among family members that can't be had without help or without a witness; sometimes we share details of the illness trajectory that a dying person cannot say for themselves. At other times, on hospice wards, we might step in as a protective boundary to prevent distress in a dying person, whose family demands are outweighing his needs as a dying man, as follows:

> Too young to die, such cases heightened the collective anxiety in the team. These were the kind of cases where urgent informal supervisions are called for. Nurses hold their breaths when entering the room, small children appear on wards reminding care staff of their own children, men and women in the primes of their lives. And here he is, riddled with cancer in his thirties, but his greatest fear it seems is of being inundated, flooded, drowned out by needy narcissistic family members. The rage in the family apartment where they all congregate is palpable, as if in a church hall, voices are raised, people squabbling about who should get the next visit to a man who can barely speak, whose thin arms and legs can no longer hold his own weight or the weight of a spoon. And in the finality of his life, he eventually learns that he has the option to say 'No' – and the team will support him in the wall that he erects, imagining perhaps that at least he will die having found his voice. As Gabor Mate (2019) tells us, sometimes the body says 'no'.

Written into our dying days

Mum is the youngest of her three sisters. There are nine years between her and her eldest, who lives only twelve miles up the motorway from her. In some ways, for many years, my mother had grown up as an only child. One sister began working in the cotton mills at fourteen when my mother was five; eventually the other left the UK, marrying a GI during the Second World War. My mother's brother, at eighteen, died of sudden peritonitis in Hong Kong, having left, perhaps escaped, home for the Army. My mother's memories of childhood are mixed. Some are hard to listen to and others are poetic: all of them form an intricate design, a piece of human cloth that coats my mother's life – a coat that at times has given her an armour, yet in the harshest of weathers it has perhaps become a little threadbare.

I hear her now, going over the stories of her past. She remembers coming home from school and crying, regularly, sitting on her mother's – a huge, wordless woman – lap and being cuddled, little said. She remembers white mice, six of them, that scurried up and down a copper pipe in one of the many homes she lived in as a little girl, her father constantly picking up and later losing jobs, which afforded them housing. These white mice, she tells me about, were real, Cinderella-like, not a figment of imagination, a hallucination from that growing GBM of hers.

She tells me about the clothes that were made by her mother, who had once been a shop-owning lady in Manchester but who had become, through marriage, a woman who scrimped and saved, sewing her own garments to see her children clothed. She tells me all of these details. I am reminded of a client, of working class descent like Mum, who resurrects all the hard times she encountered as an abused child; as a young frightened mother; as an adventurer to warmer countries. She too is trying to live in the face of the daily threat of death, presented as she is with the reality of several killer comorbidities. She tells me over and over again that her story needs to be told and here I am, the therapist, bearing witness to the patterns in her life, acknowledging the pain but also her incredible capacity to have raised children, worked, helped others, painted with what she was given in those formative years.

Silence around death was written into Mum's family, who lost the only boy abruptly. A telegram had come to the family home, a terraced house in Byfleet, an upgrade from the corrugated air-raid shelter they had once lived in on Staverton airport, a hut which her brother had left to go to war. The telegram explained that he was unwell; a second had come only hours afterwards, explaining that he was now dead, with a ruptured appendix. No one had spoken of his death, then or ever after, and the unbearable loss had been swallowed down. In 2008, with my husband and baby daughter we had finally discovered his headstone in the large hilly graveyard by Hong Kong racecourse: the sisters had been so grateful that at least one person in the family had laid flowers at his grave.

This is what my mother remembers: no tears, no open mourning, just the cracking silence of a family in pain. My grandmother had got on with her daily life, keeping the family afloat, doing the bills, making dresses, cooking stews, testing my mother on her history knowledge: able, competent but silent. Very, very silent. Her husband mourned in the only way he knew, and he drank and drank and drank, angry and angered, punishing his wife and my mother, who witnessed his rages almost every night. She was now the only child living at home, and with ferocious courage she often stood between

her father and mother in a bid to hold him back. The death
of her brother, the sadness that occupied them all, was never
mentioned. And now, as my mother faces her own death, it
stands to reason that – with her siblings at least, she is now the
youngest – she has gone quiet, secreting away the reality of
her finitude. Who am I to break this family pattern, the taboo,
the desperation of loss? And now her words, recorded on that
tiny dictaphone, sound out:

> He lost his son… all the drinking, going down to the pub
> and spending his Friday money, salary… in the pub and
> coming back late. Christmas was an absolute nightmare.
> Because he would go drinking and I would be with my
> mother (now the only child left). And we'd have a piece
> of Christmas cake and a glass of sherry, my mother and
> I, and we waited for him to come back and I was there
> for my mother. I would be there for her until he got back
> in… his temper erupted when he was drinking, yeah, I
> wasn't frightened of him, no I wasn't frightened of him.
> I have never been frightened of a man in my life. Never.
> And I never intend to be. I was a tomboy and I would
> fight back…

She tells me, clearly, categorically, that she does not want
either sister to know; I see her holding on to this sense of herself
as fearless, as a tomboy, as someone unruffled, unflappable. She
won't be seen in any other way, by them. I understand this,
not just because of their family circumstances but because I
have seen this time and time again. Many families close rank.
Some families even try to keep the truth from the person who
is dying, as a way, they argue, to protect them, a paternalistic
stance to shield them from the misery and the panic of what

is to come – even though very often, at a deeply unconscious level, a dying person knows he is dying. As Joan Didion (2012) notes, citing the work of Philippe Ariès (1991):

Neither his doctor nor his friends nor the priests... know as much about it as he. Only the dying man can tell how much time he has left. (p. 26)

He might begin to plant up all his window boxes for spring, in advance of when he usually does so. He might, like my mother, begin clearing out cupboards of his shoes and old clothes. He might, as one of my clients did, begin leaving post-it notes around the house as a way to convey his anxiety without telling anyone directly. Or leaving scribbles in his favourite books, to tell a wife how much he loves her, hoping she will find the messages when he is gone. The dying person so often knows.

Autonomies

In an end-of-life context, there can be discussions around whether or not a paternalistic approach is ever justified. In some respects this might depend on how important the patient, and/or his family, view the principle of autonomy – since autonomy acts in polarity to paternalism: one represents a sense of continued independence, the other moves into the acceptance of dependency. A paternalistic approach might assume that choices are being made in the best interest of an-Other, yet is it possible to know ever what those best interests might be – of a dying person or otherwise?

On lots of levels the concept of paternalism has negative connotations in health and social care, an arguably traditional view that the authority in medicine is located in the doctors as experts (Borgstrom et al., 2013). We now exist in times where we have become experts by experience, i.e., informal carers and patients. When to act paternalistically can be difficult to determine. For example, if a dying person has dementia and asks to be told the truth about his condition, should he be told? Some palliative care professionals may argue that withholding information is the kindest act while others may insist that a dying person must have the truth whenever he asks for it, regardless of the impact of hearing the news. Similarly, paternalism can also occur within family systems and within partnerships, and other relationships. ·

> She pauses, then meets my eye. Is this some sort of warning about how I inhabit my role as psychotherapist? 'I think he is using my illness,' she says of her husband, 'finally to control me, and to make all the decisions on my behalf. I am furious.'

For Mum, talking openly among our own immediate family unit was a must; but beyond that – among her wider network – a concealment ensued, and who were Dad and I to challenge this? What was my client's husband thinking in relation to her, and what were either party's understanding of kindness?

Open talking

I have seen mothers avoid thinking about their deaths, carrying on and making normal right up to the night they take their last breath; I have seen their husbands and teenage children push the thought out of mind, avoiding those difficult conversations, as though that will stop her death in its tracks. I have also seen the regret that follows when no one has made any preparation at all for the absence; where important things have been left unsaid; where children feel they have been cheated and memories have not been stored. I have heard of young boys and girls smashing up their bedrooms into fragments, mirroring their own internal fragmentation, after the death of a parent, unable to understand why Mum said she would 'fight this thing and get better'. And she has now let them down.

There's a lot at stake in denial, yet it must be understood, very often, as a protective response to a finality that so many of us do not wish to face.

She complains of fatigue, and a continual cold that will not go. Her nasal cavities feel constantly blocked. She has only come a few times now, and has not yet told her children that there is no treatment left available, that she is going to die. Apart from a face disfigured by surgeries, removing one and then a second tumour, this woman moves around, drives, shops, does homework when the kids come home, even keeps up with a handful of work tasks. She tries to avoid talking about dying, wants to make normal, make it go away. For the first time, she reports having discussed her death with her sister. 'I do not want to die,' she says, looking at her counsellor. 'I do not want you to die either,' the counsellor acknowledges this holding on, so understandable for a woman so young; a half-life not yet lived. These are the last words, and there will be no more. Without having left her box of memories, the letters she wished to write to her children, she dies two days after the appointment. It is quite simply too soon.

In academic circles, beyond these uniquely human micro-encounters where people employ recognisable defences and protection, we might have talked on a macro scale about living in times of death denial (Clark, 2018), a widespread cultural response to the uncomfortableness of failing, vulnerability, endings. Nonetheless, culturally perhaps this too is shifting in our western territories, with initiatives such as the Death Café movement, Dying Matters, and end-of-life doulas, with new green eco ways to celebrate death, with grieving communities memorialising the dead, with thoughts and feelings posted on Instagram and Twitter. Yet individuals – on a psychic level – can still be very private about what they wish to share about their endpoint, and the associated anxiety.

Though she is facing death head-on herself, Mum does not want to be reminded that she is dying. She wants no pity from her sisters, her vulnerabilities must be hidden from them. Her focus is on remaining the woman she recognises herself to be for as long as she can, walking around the garden taking pleasure in the birds; taking pleasure in the taste of hot chocolate; in her grandchildren and in music and, for how long we don't know, in words. And as they drop further out of sight and sound, she tells me, '*I want to stay who I am. Maintain me happy, for as long as possible, with all of you, in love.*' If this means holding on tightly to the role she has known with her sisters, then she will do so. If this means non-disclosure, this is her choice, even if I might believe that in sharing this terminal news the three sisters might forge new roles and ways of adjusting. Sometimes these ideals are founded on optimism, a belief in humanity, over and above the reality of difficult or impossible family dynamics.

Psychotherapeutic intervention can be offered to whole families, as a way into having the challenging conversations about issues no one wants to confront. In the open expression of collective vulnerability, rapprochement and connection can sometimes be found. Yet this is not always so; sometimes the histories of families are tortuous, complex, and it is simply too late to bring the closeness that may be desired but which is too precarious to navigate: this kind of coming together would mean a relinquishing of ego and defensive function, that carapace which shields us from pain of regret and from the taking of responsibility. Of course, inviting a family to think about their situation in the face of one member's dying days is not without its challenges. The general thinking in a palliative care context is that discussions around dying and death should not be avoided. Indeed, there is an assumption that if we were more open about talking about death and dying, and had the requisite skills to talk and to listen to the concerns of the dying, there would be an improvement in both end-of-life care and the experiences of bereavement (Seymour et al., 2010). What we know (Oliver, 2019) is that:

> … patients' families are far more likely to be distressed by clinical teams not explaining how sick their loved ones are, and not saying that they're dying, than by doctors openly discussing the issue and involving them in decisions. Some people won't welcome unexpected conversations about dying, however sensitively handled – but they'll be in a minority. The National Survey of Bereaved People and the National Audit of End of Life Care in Hospital make that clear, as does the Royal College of Physicians' *Talking About Dying*. Communication failings and insufficient information are a major cause of bad experiences.

Anecdotally, I have known this to be true and many patients and families are relieved that the elephant in the room is addressed with care, and an acknowledgement of the distress it causes. Anxiety, gone underground, can isolate us further from one another; death and dying unspoken can leave the patient very much alone with the end in mind. Yet it is not a failing of the healthcare professionals if those conversations cannot be had. There are patients who hold on to themselves till the last minute; patients whose veneer of strength is more important than any connection through vulnerability will ever be. Some people die without saying goodbye to anyone, until the last minute convincing everyone that the illness will be defeated – the bereaved are then left with an unshakeable guilt that they were not able to express all the things that mattered, all the gratitude they felt. We know that families can collude with a patient's denial, and we might ask ourselves who will benefit from disturbing that protection? Families, all together, can shut down, their systems closed and panicked by the notion of help, and transparency; other families limp from crisis to crisis, unable to stop enough to do the reflection work that may allow for some calm. A professional prompting such difficult conversations can be seen as an intrusive object, puncturing an altogether more heroic outlook that the entire family clings to.

Yet there are times in my work where the counselling space offered to siblings, children, mothers and fathers makes room for the mourning work that is to come, allows people to see how closely attached they are to the person dying, and thus how closely attached they are to an imaginary positive outcome.

Two sisters and two brothers, angry that their father is no longer taking food and drink, making accusations that the consultants and nursing staff are cutting their dad's life short; their dad, a fighter, who has only just been withdrawn from potentially life-saving clinical trials. It can't be, this quick demise. One daughter is so angry but when her tears finally erupt, the anger is simple. 'I will miss him,' she says, an awareness, gradual, that her father's body is shutting down. Brother, his father's lookalike, pulls out a cider and a packet of crisps in the counselling room, as if he is down the pub, machismo disguising pain, which gives way simply to care: 'What about a lollypop for him, anything but starving?'. The second son is silent, too hard to speak or to think perhaps. And then the wisdom that comes with being the older sister, recently too a mother of her father's first grandchild, 'But that lolly won't keep him alive for us, you know.' There they are, siblings clustered around the impending loss of dad; experiencing for the first time a relief from anger, a sense of falling down the rabbit hole, into a sadness that had not yet been borne.

For our family unit, though, Mum's death has not been evaded, we have talked and talked and talked. Of course, in end-of-life care, there may be times when functional conversations about people's preferences take place; and also conversations involved in deep emotional support and empathy. My mother seemed to appreciate both: to be able to get her affairs in order was as important to her as being able to replay any regrets or hopes she had for those who would outlive her. The ability to listen, to ask questions that were open-ended, to give her space for exploration was vital; really hearing a dying person can make so much difference to the way that someone ends their days. You may remember the young man who requested that no unwanted visitors, even family members, slip into his room when he was dying; without careful attuned listening his death would have been an anxious flooded one; in the end he achieved just a little peace. My mother, too, has chosen her room, albeit metaphorical, and the people she wishes to have in it.

We talk a lot about patient autonomy in palliative care. Autonomy is one of the principles in the ethical framework proposed by Beauchamp and Childress (2009), two ethicists interested in ethical issues emerging in clinical settings, which were also being discussed politically and academically in the 1980s in America. This was partially in response to a series of unexpected deaths of participants in medical experiments, which raised concerns about the ethical context of the trials. Understandably, then, Beauchamp and Childress's work stemmed from a desire to create ethical guidance around decision-making in clinical experience, and practice, and in medical research. Four principles of ethical decision-making were identified, namely: beneficence, non-maleficence, autonomy and justice.

Of course, applying these principles in practice is not always straightforward, the model itself critiqued on the grounds that it reflects an overarching Anglo-centric discourse individualistic in nature (Turner, 2009). Relatedly, Gillon (2003) suggested that respect for autonomy is the most important principle, again linked in healthcare contexts to individual choice and control (Corrigan, 2003). We know, in some societies, the interests of the wider group, the collective, takes precedence, which indicates just how westernised the four principles are (Kelley et al., 2010; Johnstone and Kanitsaki, 2009; Back and Huak, 2005).

Indeed autonomy, as a guiding principle, is one that often features prominently in the notion of a 'good death'. In hospice meetings across the UK, we might find professionals making associations between patient choice (place of death, advance directives fulfilled) and a good death. As Meltzer (2018) says, 'dying well is a defining obsession of our time.' It is certainly an obsession of mine, now, as Mum becomes more unwell.

Yet, though I recognise the problematic nature of foregrounding autonomy and choice, it seems that for her –

glioblastoma eroding her cognitive capacities – to maintain a sense of self, it is vitally important that we make every attempt to support her decisions as they shift and change throughout this illness.

Choice and control: is it that simple?

For now, my mother has asked my father to act as a boundary around her. She has also decided on the biopsy route, a source of anxiety for all of us since the date for this investigation is still not forthcoming. She has chosen not to eat or drink when her words finally fail her; she has decided that her body be carted off for medical research, that her corneas be taken, that her body be cremated, no funeral, with ashes to be sprinkled around the old mulberry tree in my parents' garden; she has decided on a Louis MacNeice poem to be read by my husband. All this is her, it has meaning, her meaning, stamped all over it. She is a person for whom her personal autonomy is vital and she holds to it with unending strength and force. All the critical thinking, the analysis of ethical concepts, the attempt to balance carefully one principal with another, will do nothing to avert her from making her own decisions.

She remembers a mulberry tree she loved as a child. She remembers its fruits, so luscious and bountiful, its constancy, a constancy she did not have as a small girl when she and her siblings were ripped from homes and moved about. Mum wants to be spread by our mulberry tree – the one she and Dad planted – at the bottom of their garden. Given the lack of control she had as a child, I begin to see why control and autonomy are such pressing concerns for her. In a paradoxical way, we might say that, by making her choices now, the process of dying becomes somehow life affirming. She cannot be plunged back into the chaos, the out-of-controlness of those lost worlds of childhood. And here I am, seeing that for my mother this problematic discourse of 'choice and control'[1], at this stage in her disease progression, while she has language and cognition, fits.

It is funny because there is a universal symbolism that we give to trees, one of solidity, and perhaps individuation. We know that trees are grounded in the earth, yet their branches move and sway with the wind around them; leaves drop and disintegrate, the trunk stretches and grows. For Jung, the tree could be seen as a metaphor for the self and, as Wohlleben (2018) points out, trees are also relational, meeting and communicating with the roots of other species beneath the ground. My mother, in these final weeks of her life, seems to be both grounded and rooted in our home yet journeying into another state of consciousness that resides in nature: she is both becoming herself and losing herself simultaneously; the choices she makes are perhaps the last acts of the human egoic self that she will make.

However, she does not make her decisions lightly, in isolation: '… the exercise of judgement is rarely a solitary undertaking… Deciding for oneself is not something that one typically does by oneself' (Martin & Hickerson, 2013). Choice is often relational. Exploring and problematising the personalisation agenda in social care, Sowerby (2010) makes it clear that the way that choice is constructed in neoliberal policy lets us all down. Even those of us who are relatively independent need a compassionate ear at times and, more so, those who are moving into an experience of greater dependency. Choice is often not an isolated activity for one; it is embedded in dialogue and conversation – a process that moves from the internal to

---

[1] For instance, Voice, Choice and Control, 2015; Care Act, 2014; Living Well with Dementia: National Dementia Strategy, 2009; Putting People First, 2007

the external and back again until conclusions are made. Indeed we have ideas about what we wish to do – the new job, car, holiday – and most of us tend to run such decisions past others.

In these days with Mum, she sounds out my father and I, checking our tone and facial expressions, as well as our words, to see what we think. Yet both he and I also understand that Mum needs to be in the driving seat, as this tumour grows and will eventually give her no choice about which words will remain intact and which will go.

In order to see what it is that Mum wants in terms of treatment plans, the way she wants to live out her day to day life, we have to have those conversations that reference the end: death is our framework. Despite the reality that the precision of my mother's thinking mind is a little off, there is something about looking death in the eye that gives her clarity about how she wants to spend her every last minute. Some moments are simple ones. She chooses to do short walks with my father. She wants to see our children and cuddle them close. She also wants to accept death and, at the same time, try to stay alive. Despite the likelihood of her limited time, she holds out hope for extra time and says that she will embark on whatever is the most aggressive form of treatment available to her. Her line of reasoning perplexes me: she begins to position herself as a guinea pig, helping out the medical profession as a sort of research participant, even though the treatments she will opt for are not experimental… Somehow we see that this gives her meaning, and there is no use in puncturing that reality for now. It's as if she wants to give her life up for knowledge production; there is hope, the hope of leaving one's mark.

We do not put her right, and perhaps this is the moment of change. Our omission of the truth is a sort of psychic paternalism: a cover-up job that covers Mum in a sequence of beliefs that her death will not go unnoticed, that she will have made an impact. Which of course she has done, but which perhaps doesn't seem quite enough. For her, at least.

Dying people often start to scramble around in their dying days to try to make something of themselves, fearing that it is too late to make their mark. People scribble notes, decide to finish uncompleted PhDs, get to islands on the edge of civilisation, knit egg cosies in mass bulk for charities. My mother knew that she had improved the lives of students, that she had been a good enough mother and wife, and special cuddly grandmother, but I was curious about this need of hers to give her life – albeit in fantasy – to medical science, that final act of generosity and value. For young people who are dying, the anxiety of wasted time can be much more apparent and painful to bear witness to, and often that anxiety seeps into family members and staff teams caring for them.

> He has booked several holidays now in the hope that he will complete his bucket list of travelling around the world. Each session is filled with another adventure, ticking off grizzly bears, mountain climbs, waterfalls. We try to get underneath the manic activity but he is not there yet. He says that he has been researching engineering papers and is going to try to write for publication, even though the yellowing of his eyes tell me that he has little time left. He will try to get the kitchen completed for his wife, and wants to buy her a new car. And then he sighs, and we talk about his exhaustion. 'I won't be able to do it all; time is running out.'

Beneath this relentlessness of doing, the productiveness so valued in capitalist economies, is the fear that when I stop I no longer exist. In psychotherapeutic interventions in palliative care, we might often be attempting to think about being, about the continuance of living – in the smaller, less recognised, or overtly valued, moments of the everyday. As Atul Gawande (2015) puts it:

> [T]ry to figure out what living a life really means to you under the circumstances… This is the consequence of a society that faces the final phase of the human life cycle by trying not to think about it. We end up with institutions that address any number of societal goals… but never the goal that matters to the people who reside in them: how to make life worth living when we're weak and frail and can't fend for ourselves anymore. (p. 77)

These questions are ones we sometimes avoid; they force us to look at our dependence on others, thus forcing us to consider the terms of human sociability. We might come to know that the speeding up of our time on this vast planet prevents us from recognising small, simple, spontaneous acts of humanity.

LIVING PLANS: HEROICS

'It is a tragedy that most of us die before
we have begun to live.'

Erich Fromm (1990-1980)

Much to our dismay, Mum changes her mind. She states categorically that she does not want chemo. Some forms of chemo are equated with hair loss, something she dreads. As a small girl she was riddled with nits twice, she tells me, her hair cut back making her look boyish and unpleasant. I have seen the photographs of a young girl, her hair bluntly and untidily cropped, and wearing an obviously hand-sewn dress. She tells me of another time in her early life when she was made to wear a skull cap, because large flakes of skin were falling from her head. Eczema, psoriasis, welts, we might imagine, but she doesn't clarify. Due to the cruelty of children, she was teased for wearing it at school.

Shame and authenticity

Over seventy years later, this shame still haunts her. She will not be subjected to such humiliation again. Even if her life depends on it. Of course, to us, her hair is immaterial; it is life we want to preserve. Hers. Hair loss is not an option; she is firm. To know someone is at least in part, to understand them, to accept their choices, however difficult they may be for us to bear: there are always aspects of another human being which show themselves to you, take you by surprise. In these days of my mother's illness and her increasing weakness, the slowing down, there are fewer moments where we seem to exist together on the surface. Of course, she still applies mascara, wants the small ticking watch on a chain that dangles from her neck, asks me to pass the small discreet shaving machine that she uses for the whiskers on her chin. But overall this is a time in her life where she seems to explain herself, her actions, her choices, in relation to different pockets of her own personal history. Each choice, each sentence uttered penetrates depths of her that hitherto I had known little about, and so here it is – the gifts that we receive when we look death squarely in the face. As de Hennezel (1997) writes, in her tender account of working as a hospice psychologist in Paris:

> [N]o human being can be reduced to what we see, or think we see. Any person is infinitely larger, and deeper, than our narrow judgements can discern... He or she can never be considered to have uttered the final word on anything, is always developing, always has the power of self-fulfillment, and a capacity for self-transformation through all the crises and trials of life. (p. 19)

In a professional palliative care setting, our deep sense of attunement to a patient, those moments in which he shares with you his secrets, can at times minimise his or her total pain (Saunders, 1964) even in those instances where someone is raging in the face of impending death.

He is angry, angry about his illness and about his life choices, driven by gain and not by friendship. 'Psychologists, psychiatrists, all the psycho people, they're all charlatans.' He knows he gives her a hard time, but this is life force and a test. For a dying man. She knows he has to keep her on her toes; she knows she has to be alongside him in his rage. It's so hard to trust her, yet each week he tells her – this charlatan who bears his hatred and aggression – another one of those secrets he has yet to unearth before he dies. One day, a week before he succumbs to the threat of breathlessness, he apologises for having been so 'negative'. She queries this, 'Have you?' she asks. Unusually directive, and sounding a little esoteric, she says, 'Perhaps by categorising your angry feelings this way, you are closing yourself down. What if we were simply curious about what you call negative? Would we not find hurt, pain and suffering there instead?' His eyes drift, as if taking flight to memories past before returning to his lonely present. Moments later, he will admit that perhaps this woman, who has been trying to see him, has at last become a friend. And though at times he has exhausted her no end, and that together they had only found glimpses of his gentler soul, she will miss him.

De Hennezel's words echo in my mind as I discover that Mum has changed her tune about chemo. She has mulled it over, and spoken with the neuro-oncology nurse, whom she trusts. The nurse, A, tells her that TMZ, the possible chemo she might be offered, has no hair loss side effects. The hauntings of the playground dissipate. Mum is reassured, returning to her original decision. The biopsy is back on the table once again in order that we explore the possibility of the tumour being chemo-responsive or not. Living with a terminal condition – working out which treatment to embark on and which to reject – is difficult to navigate. Anxieties mount and time ebbs away, as we try to make sense of what is on offer. Early experiences in life, or the hauntings of family members who have been ill, can side-track us and prevent us from moving forward. I have known clients to refuse all forms of treatment, and reject appointment dates with consultants because of traumatic memories associated with particular hospitals – the scars of being on psychiatric wards, or having lost babies there, parents fatally ill. In instances like these, for example, counselling in a palliative care context might be the first time someone has been offered the opportunity to come to terms with earlier tragedies or losses. Sometimes, the aim of counselling is simply to support someone to understand their choices better, so that there is greater clarity around the unconscious blocks that might be preventing them from a longer life, or more appropriate treatment.

This is why choice has to be understood as a relational activity. Mum had been in discussion with Dad and me for several days, and subsequently sounded out her thoughts with A, the neuro-oncology nurse. This is a web, a system, with the professional voice mediating – oftentimes – between different members. A provided the knowledge and, though I was by no means acting as my mother's psychotherapist, being able to listen to her stories of shame and bullying made space enough for her to give some thought to asking further questions.

Often a psychotherapist in palliative care functions as the keeper of tales, as I have already noted. We are there to hear a story unfold: no clever interventions, no reassurances, almost a human attic with chambers in our minds of life fragments offered up in trust. In line with de Hennezel's (1997) words, 'How could one not be powerfully moved when one is the silent witness to that most solemn moment when a human being glimpses the approach of death?' And so it is.

At times, though, my mother expresses herself as if she is Lord Gautama: a local yoga teacher tells me that recording her wisdom is a must-do. These moments, where she speaks from a place of her own personal learning, a culmination of what she has discovered since knowing she has a brain tumour yet simultaneously known all along, seem to help us all. At base, it is her generosity that helps. Without taking away from the anticipatory grief that we are experiencing, and the quiet tears that surface each day, there are curiously rich rewards from speaking and being with Mum. As Gatewood (2010) asks, providing a model of spiritual care which seeks to find constructive meaning out of anticipatory grief and drawing on the work of Viktor Frankl:

> Does death completely cancel out meaning? No. Frankl explains: 'As the end belongs to the story, so death belongs to life. If life is meaningful, then it is so whether it is long or short.'. (Frankl, 1967, p. 128; Gatewood, p.146)

At times Mum tries to recite the poems she learned at grammar school; sometimes she can't recall them and revises them with her own lines. One morning she puts every effort into repeating the last verse from Henry Wadsworth's 'The Day is Done'.

> And the night shall be filled with music,
>
> And the cares, that infest the day,
>
> Shall fold and fade away.

The final line is her own, accepting one.

Perhaps this is to protect us all from the unbearableness of her dying. Yet I also imagine that this good grace of hers is indeed a final act of care, a final act of magnanimity. Gatewood (2010) states:

> One is free to take a stand. One cannot control conditions, but one can determine one's stance toward those conditions. Finitude is a condition of human living, but one can, and should, anticipate that condition and take a stand relative to one's finitude. (p. 148)

Throughout history, writers and philosophers have examined the link between one's approach to death and to life. As therapist Stanley Keleman (1974) writes: 'The character of our life is the character of our dying; both are part of one process.'

Of course it is tempting to suggest Mum has become all light, all goodness, a woman who might make a gentle departure. There are other dimensions to her, though, as there were in life. Not least, she is a woman with a brain tumour, who at times becomes distanced and out of reach. Sometimes she cannot follow us, with our explanations of a day's routines or the care she is being offered. It is at times like this that it becomes almost impossible to discuss her treatment plans with her: Mum is either forgetful, or she is unable to retain the medical words that are being thrust upon her. She gets frustrated and wants to shut down, go into herself where perhaps she feels safer, or less stupid, a place where she can pretend none of this is happening.

Medicalisation of death

My father calls me, asking me to make contact with the neurology nurse, A, as he feels that there are still loose threads about Mum's treatment floating in the air. The biopsy still has not been scheduled, and he is becoming anxious. My mother is cross in the background of the telephone call, stating – no messing – that the nurse knows how she is going to proceed. It is hard to know if the 'she' is Mum or the nurse; whichever it is, there is a sense that Mum implicitly trusts A. This is an example of the way that the care that professionals offer is not simply about efficiency and capability, but about the way that individuals form attachments with them; or project on to nurses, doctors, psychotherapists, nursing assistants identities – borrowed from the valleys of interior space – both good and bad, trusting or abandoning, abrupt or humane.

'Biopsy, biopsy, biopsy,' Mum shouts angrily, pushing her words out in the hope they may land somewhere, that Dad and I will receive them and honour her wishes. Yet Dad is sure that the nurse is still expecting a confirmation call. In instances like this, it becomes clear that navigating the system is not always easy: Dad, in his eighties, unsure of the correct channels of communication, and my mother – as has always been the case – believes she knows what is happening. I sense the tension and split between them: these are the moments that children often step in, whether they are young or old, whether there is a terminal illness or not; somehow children try to make the tensions better.

Mum has always prided herself on her memory, one which has historically retained the minutiae of any event. She continues in this vein, yet Dad can see that her memory is far from sharp now.

This is not just about older people, though. There are plenty of younger people within my work who, in an understandable state of heightened anxiety, find it hard to work out what is the best course of action, and which professional is the most helpful contact. Working with couples, there is often one who becomes the chaser, following up appointments, pushing for more scans, while the other holds themselves together in their illness trajectory. Yet here, between Mum and Dad, the lines were blurring and I was beginning to sense their collective shakiness.

In relation to the monolith of hospital departments, or where treatments themselves have been split between different consultants, different hospitals, there are patients who begin to talk about themselves as if they have become part-object formations: a kidney will be treated in urology, the cancer by the oncologist in another hospital, a surgeon to perform a biopsy elsewhere. Beneath these cold, practical explanations of where they will go, and which organ will be treated first, is the sense of a human being screaming out, waiting to be noticed as a whole object.

> 'I am a complex case,' she says. 'I know I am complex, and so I am having to learn to ask that people remember who I am too; that I have a son I want to live for, that I am worried about his exams and that I need to live till then.'

Medical curative treatment of patients has an altogether different quality to a palliative approach, which has at its centre the ethos of a holistic responsiveness to each individual. In the care of the dying, the focus is more explicitly on the human first and the meaning and comfort of that life, given that it is a limited one. The former is of course about human life, and saving it, but the focus is on the organ that will kill or the disease that will shorten a life. Being treated medically, heroics – a focus on saving – are understandably still at play; a person may at times be broken down into different areas of treatment: body parts, cellular activity and so forth.

The medicalisation of death and dying, as it might be termed, is embedded in western cultural practice. The establishment of the General Register Office and an official system for registering births and deaths through the Births and Deaths Registration Act 1836 (Rugg, 1999) heralded the increasing medicalisation of death in the United Kingdom. By law all deaths must be officially registered and documented. If there are any concerns about the death, the coroner is involved in order to establish whether the death was due to natural or unnatural causes (Howarth, 2007). As a result of these statutory requirements, dating back to the mid-nineteenth century, death is now a formally medicalised event in the life span of each individual.

Interestingly, despite such official practices, there is a sense that in western cultures, a widespread death avoidance has run parallel to this. Ironically, even the western funeral industry is considered by some to obfuscate death and loss in a way that separates the living from death; it has been accused of shutting down ritual, thus representing the untouchable, feared nature of death in contemporary society. Caitlin Doughty (2017) writes:

> What's more, due to the corporatisation and commercialism of deathcare, we have fallen behind the rest of the world when it comes to proximity, intimacy, and ritual around death. (p. 15)

Medical knowledge and healthcare services are arguably drawn into this societal anxiety, also representative of the view that death should be avoided, resisted or at least postponed

(Clark, 2002). Beyond that, patients are often constructed as consumers and so the medical profession itself is at the behest of service users who demand that they live longer. When death does take place, following treatment, such an outcome can at times be seen as the failure of medicine, technology and science – a network of interdependent public and private services – rather than as a natural progression of a particular disease trajectory. Here we enter into another overarching discourse of our time, the fear of failure. This sense of failure – the clinical trials that don't work, the chemo that has broken someone down further, etc. – does help us to understand, perhaps, why medical practitioners will occasionally treat someone so aggressively; particularly with patients who may unconsciously communicate a desperation to stay alive or a deep-seated fear of dying.

The rabid quest to prolong life is often the subject of much political debate. We know of surgical procedures that may be performed on already weak and fragile people whose quality of life might deteriorate post-operatively. The tension among the medical community between heroism and stoicism in the treatment of people with terminal conditions is a theme in Atul Gawande's *Being Mortal*. As Gawande (2015), a US surgeon, writer and public health researcher, noted:

> *I learned a lot of things in medical school, but mortality wasn't one of them … The way we saw it, and the way our professors saw it, the purpose of medical schooling was to teach how to save lives, not how to tend to their demise.* (p.1)

In a medical setting, death and dying may well be conceptualised as technical problems in need of solving, yet in her advanced years, and with her poor health, the surgeons and oncologists responsible for my mother's care are realistic that a brutal regime of treatment was likely to be high risk, resulting in the diminishment of her quality of life. The subtext to these discussions was that it would be better to prepare for dying than for living, and to enjoy the time that each day held.

The neurosurgeon, whom we had met early on, had said, laughingly, 'It is a fiction we tell ourselves that we are all going to live forever, but tomorrow I too could be knocked down by a bus, so how would any of us use our time knowing that?' Mum, it was clear, was terminal.

Navigating systems

Nonetheless, she had decided on a sort of midway treatment option. She had wanted to buy time, where possible. In the absence of a date for the biopsy Mum gets one step closer to death, though. Dad's anxiety is palpable, partially in response to my mother's increasing outbursts, and I rattle around in my own brain trying to find the right words to calm him, to soothe him. In the end, I write an email to A, the neuro-nurse, asking that a date be expedited, and cc-ing Dad, so that he can read to Mum. Sometimes, in the midst of precariousness, we want someone to do the thinking and doing for us. Relationships work like this, shifts between symmetry and asymmetry all along the course of a life, of lives, together. When we care for each other, we – quite simply – learn how to turn take, to adapt, reversing long established patterns so an-Other gets a look in of care that they may have provided for you.

Mum is not surprised that she doesn't have a date for her biopsy yet. 'We are waiting for a slot.' She seems to be oblivious to the anxiety that Dad is carrying, and in some ways this is not new. Of the two, she has always been the more casual, but now the tumour itself makes her cut-offness to fears that linger more pronounced.

Sometimes I believe Mum when she says she knows what the pathway is, and sometimes I am a little more dubious. It is hard to distinguish when she knows, and when she is compensating for what she simply doesn't know anymore. Like a person living with dementia, whose memories form and reform like shifting sand, it is hard to tell what Mum is genuinely recalling these days. At times she confabulates to hide her cognitive losses: a way to protect us and her from the reality of the effects of a growing mass of cells pressing down on her brain.

Whether she can follow the complexity of the possible treatment plan I am unsure, but what is clear and unswerving is that she is not parting with her own voice just yet. Though she may be baffled by all these new forms of language – chemo or radiotherapy, biopsy, steroid, advance care planning, anti-seizure, GBM – and the way that time seems to have become elastic, her intuition, albeit inconsistent, remains.

Children and loss

When someone is dying some families intentionally set out to spend as much time together as possible – this can range from short trips away, en masse, to regular visits to the family home. Of course this is not always the case, some children of ailing parents keep their distance; the thought of a parent dying can be overwhelming. It is not unheard of in larger families that one sibling might take up the role of carer – particularly in families where there has been a divorce or one parent remains alone – while the other siblings, perhaps living abroad, dial in for updates or do an intense stint of helping before returning to their own frantic lives.

Like adults, an acknowledging empathetic other is an important supportive presence for a grieving child – someone who makes room for his upset and makes a place available where he does not have to be so strong.

So caught up am I in mourning the death of my mother's relationship with the children that a jagged sense of guilt plays on, and more so because I don't allow the beauty of Eloise's sweet young voice to be fully felt. Ann Aragno (2003), who movingly writes about her own experience of grief, and reworking the psychoanalytic paradigm beyond Freud's decathexis, states: 'Time stands still for the grief-stricken.' Though her conceptualisation follows the first year after a death, for me in that moment time stood still, the only place I could exist in was an imagined aching future in which a painful final severance acted as an obstacle to joy.

Two days later, my daughter and I walk to school, and she points out that every year her Mama has bought her one of these coats, like the one she is wearing – a fur-lined bomber jacket which covers her on this icy morning. 'Next year, she'll buy me other one,' she says, then stops, checking herself, makes eye contact with me, checks my response, recognising somewhere between us both – in this dislocating space of knowing and quite-knowing – that this is unlikely to be the case. 'That is a thought,' I say, a little choked but not wishing to unsettle before the school day begins. She continues, 'and Bear' – her brother's nickname – 'can have this one,' she says, hoping Mama will replenish her wardrobe and the coats will be ever down the line; a symbolic external object that might come to represent something of the memories, a passing Mama's dialogue and story, a sensory inner reality that fully be shared. We smile, together, and walk on. My think, would have done *anything, anything for you* two.

In our very small unit, already a family that kept in touch and saw one another freely, a more concerted and conscious effort was made to visit Mum. During one particular weekend, she proved that her intuition was still very much intact. Again the similarities between the effects of her glioblastoma and a condition like dementia seemed to overlap: with both, despite cognitive decline and greater difficulties with the simple tasks of daily living, a deep emotional sensitivity, a primordial capacity for felt-sense-making, continued.

I had asked my ten-year-old daughter, Eloise, to take a few minutes to perform a song from *Oliver*, a local amateur production. Mum repeats from time to time that she wants to survive until the first performance, only two months away. We still don't know what two months from now will look like. Seeing her granddaughter take to the stage is worth living for, reminding her of her own childhood self, no doubt, devouring English literature and dramatic verse. Fearing that Mum won't be around I had packed the *Oliver* script, hoping Eloise might do a small intimate performance in advance, my own need to bring joy to a dying woman. Here I was wheeling my daughter out, trademarks of the narcissistic parent, to do her thing. I began to notice a tension in myself, attempting to disentangle all the real and imagined needs between us as a family. I sat in discomfort, wanting to help to create a perfect moment yet angered with myself for the pressure I was generating; my daughter was understandably awkward and unwilling.

Sensing the pressure of her mother, Eloise twisted the sleeves of her navy blue cardigan around her fingers. Even this seemed at odds with the quirky, unselfconscious little girl she was fast becoming. It was as if she understood the seriousness, communicated by me, of this closed-group performance in front of her gran. She stood paralysed. I wanted to scream out loud,

'There isn't any time for delay', that Mum might not make it to *Oliver*. And yet I hated myself for sacrificing Eloise, as if her singing alone would keep Mum alive.

It was my mother, the woman who had always pushed me to achieving grades and qualifications I had no interest in, who whispers, so gently, from the corner of the room: 'Darling, only do it if you want to.' At this point, I push back in my chair and hit my own head hard on the wall behind me; as if my brain too is exploding under the tightness of this moment, and the culmination of weeks of anticipatory grief. Tears rise up in my eyes; tears too in my daughter's eyes, and there is a silent realisation – too intense fully to assimilate – that this might be one of the last times we are together, and it is beyond difficult to bear.

'Things are turning out well this morning,' says Dad, dryly, who notices that my son has curled himself up, foetal, on the hospital bed that my mother now uses, he is too fragile and in need of care. This bed, this site of care, frailty, decline, will shortly be empty of Mum and there will be no more performances for her to see; and yet we will all go on to watch them, imagining her response as if she were there.

I look at my daughter, and reiterate my mother's words, 'Tinks,' I say, 'it's okay, it's my fault. Mama loves your singing too but you don't need to...' With that, she begins, 'I'll do anything... for you dear, anything...'

My mother and daughter look at each other, smiling. This bond has been a strong one, and it is such a sadness that this important relationship will only live on in the emotional realm once her grandmother is gone. Experiencing the death of a close relative is no less painful for a child than it is for an adult; and depending on the age can be all the more confusing. Children under the age of six, it is said, are not able to grasp the permanence of death and may ask when someone is coming

back. Death is experienced as an absence, but the finality of it is too great a loss to comprehend. Only much later might a child explain that, as a three-year-old, he knew that his grandfather had died but had not understood that he wouldn't come to any more of his birthday parties.

Children may not always formulate in words how they are feeling, but may enact the emotional turmoil through behaviour an appearance of clinging, or adhesive relating; angry disrupti outbursts or blank expressions of denial. Children might quickly switch off a powerful feeling, so overwhelming is i engross themselves in play. Adults may mistake this as a si they are fine or don't care, but sometimes this underes the complexity of a child's emotional world.

Beyond this, children through life take their cues from their parents, and it is no different in emotionally brittle family culture will generate guarded responses, angry parental grievers, angry so forth. Sometimes children also take up the in relation to a grieving parent, masking thei splitting off their own vulnerability in orde person who also needs to support them.

In that instant in the study, both my c' – were experiencing their own sense of I was under no illusion that I too was upon them; my own anxieties about lo with a gaping grandparental void.

Children shift and change, dem and different behaviours as they a growing, new anxieties emerge In relation to grief, then, a ch to process grief differently to separating and individuating.

The intimacies and relentlessness of care and being a carer

The theme of care – that commitment to another human being, the possibility of losing oneself in the all-encompassing needs of others – emerges and re-emerges during the course of the weeks that follow. My father and mother, though good friends, have in many ways lived separate lives. Despite a shared value system, a left-leaning political stance, they tend to fill their heads with different things. The cottage in which they have lived for many years has in some ways been neatly divided. Mum has mostly taken the back end of the house, the main lounge and a conservatory that opens out onto the flatter stretch of the garden, at the end of which grows a beautiful catalpa tree and an area dug out to accommodate my father's vegetable patch. Dad has taken up residence in the front, just beyond the kitchen, in his bijoux study where he reigns over his old, old computer and keyboard, the erratic printer, and television that feeds him news from across the world. His room looks out onto a small pond and beyond down further, on a hilly slope, to the mulberry tree under which Mum wishes her ashes to be thrown.

But now, since 'the silly thing' has come into their lives, the space between them has closed. Though there are some hours in the day when Mum takes root again in her lounge area, Dad retreating to his files and keyboard, they come together more often. Dad has started to sit with Mum, guiding her through the crossword – hard, cryptic ones – that she once did with ease. Nowadays she is simply delighted if she can retrieve one or two of the words, phrases, anagrams that once sprang so readily from her lucid brain. Dad has downloaded a crossword app on his telephone, and reports how good this activity has been for the both of them.

There is much worth in taking our need for intimacy seriously, particularly if it has been difficult to find a way to connect with others. Therapists often discuss the value of sharing vulnerabilities, finding ways to be more conscious of our triggers so that a partner or friend may understand moments of conflict or tension we may re-enact, which can often be put right with loving attention. All of this of course is invaluable and brings us closer to one another, sometimes even on the therapeutic coach.

Most of us, though, are living in the humdrum realities of the everyday, working, getting kids to school, making dinners, putting bins out, and so our lives do not always slow down enough for intensely conscious intimate encounters – not always. And so I begin to wonder if most of us are putting too much pressure on ourselves to become so deeply attuned, because intimate connection can also be easy, you can slide into it and it becomes part of the quotidian. It's just a case of noticing it: sometimes a child might grab your hand and ask you to check if the aisles in the local supermarket are configured in the same way that the same brand of supermarket was on his holiday. If we step into this moment and playfully check the aisles with him, the experience validated and together, so simple, there is a shared moment – a way into conversation, to memory, to mischief. For some reason, I felt enormous pride in my parents as they smoothly found ways into developing new patterns of intimacy, nothing grandiose, no long held gazes and heavy honest conversation, but the easy moments where they laughed at the words being made up with the crossword app, Dad compromising and Mum acknowledging his coming forward to be *with* her.

In the work I do, it becomes clear that many couples – when one is faced with a life-limiting illness – can no longer embark on physical intimacies once enjoyed and sometimes both are speaking a different language (the carer may be pragmatic, understandably embedded in the material; the 'patient' may very occasionally become zen-like, spiritual, sometimes as a way of escaping to a plane more bearable than the stuckness of debilitating illness). Yet there are intimacies among them, spontaneous and unaffected – it is kept in the humour they share, the laughter and lightness, which of course might hide their pain yet can so often keep people close.

So what is this? It's to say that good enough intimate moments are found cleaning our teeth together in that split second where we might pull a funny face in the bathroom mirror; it is about collecting shells and comparing their shapes and sizes; it is about gentle teasing, banter; it is in picking up the leaves from the garden and carrying them to the compost heap together and of course it is in touch and talking. But if we are sometimes able to tread lightly together, even at the most difficult times, human connection just happens when we aren't even looking for it. Without too much thought. Every day.

Dad had never been able to understand my mother's love of crosswords, her need to prove that she still had it, that her linguistic synapses were still firing. When I stop to think about it, as people often do with hindsight, I wonder if Mum's claim that she had such a good memory was a defensive strategy, a cover-up job, to avoid some untold, unspoken anxiety about her brain.

'Ess,' Dad says to me, recognising gradually his own need to be close to her, 'I think Mum needs me near her.' He couldn't be more right, and I worry that he might feel regretful that he hadn't done the crossword with his wife more often. I worry that we all might regret the missed opportunities of joining our individual universes together, orbiting more frequently around each other's interests before settling again on our own. Getting the balance between enmeshment and distance demands real effort in families, the former either overbearing for the dying person or, in reverse, too thin and unsupportive. In hospice wards throughout the country, there will be families where the dynamics – split off from conscious thought – cause terrible psychic pain for all concerned.

> She has withdrawn into herself, mute, unspeaking. She stares up at the ceiling from her bed. The husband says nothing, reads his book as if nothing has changed. Daughters, both of them, offering an occasional visit. Only the son – borne of an earlier, shorter and unsatisfactory relationship – notices that his mother is distancing herself from everyone. 'She doesn't feel that we are there for her,' he says, echoing his own feelings about the way this family has treated him. 'Can't you all see that she is like a baby, scared, staring at the ceiling?' He is becoming incensed at the way everyone is turning a blind eye to what is going on. His intuition is striking yet he appears crazed, such is the impermeability of this family, which avoids all moves towards closeness.

My father, who has always held himself in by intellect, is increasingly recognising need at a profoundly emotional level. In new ways, ways most unexpected to me and perhaps to him, too, he shows that he will also do *anything, anything* for Mum. Even, finally, the crossword. These are the strange compromises we make for one another, some so simple, to uphold intimacy.

At the beginning of January, following the devastating seizure Mum had had on Boxing Day, she was moved to a specialist hospital, with four different colour-coded neuroscience wards, so that a biopsy on her tumour could be performed. It was unclear at that point what kind of tumour we were dealing with and, though benign tumours can be life-threatening, we had held out hope for one without malignancy. Though Mum had stayed in hospital for several days then, awaiting the biopsy, it had been decided by the MDT (multi-disciplinary team) in the hospital that, given her age and health and by now the suspected aggressiveness of the cancer, she be given a chance to mull over the need or not for a biopsy. Immediately, I had sensed the gravity of the situation. Dad had shed tears on hearing the news, so was seemingly aware on some pre-conscious level, but his conscious mind didn't allow him to articulate what some part of him knew, not for weeks after. Mum was stunned into silence, but had immediately got to work on thinking about how to proceed. What was common for us all was that everyone was in fact relieved that Mum could finally go home. The stay in hospital, the continual waiting, the sense of displacement was too much for two older people, whose daily routines and the familiarity of home gave a structure and meaning to their lives. In some ways the team was right to offer up time for reflection, yet in me – as someone younger with children, a potentially rich future ahead – another series of thoughts were bubbling beneath the surface. My sense of impatience was palpable – the living with not-knowing, the absence of definitiveness – and I wondered about all those younger people, parents of small children, who push and push for treatment, who split off the reality of death until that last minute. I could understand just how hard the news of a terminal illness must be to assimilate for young families in this situation. Nonetheless, I also believe in retrospect that I was holding on to this sense of a frustration of waiting for our family, and as we continued to wait – whether it was Mum and Dad at home, expecting an appointment letter or the sense of suspended time in hospital reception areas – it became clear that the impatience moved around between us. It is not uncommon to notice that powerful feelings often attributed to one member of the family tend – when we pay close attention to it – to circulate among people, and the clear demarcation of where feelings belong begin to blur beyond the initial and obvious valencies that one individual might have over another.

Nonetheless, a period of reflection, which in our case was offered up following what you might imagine to have been a thoughtful multi-disciplinary team meeting, allowed for space for some difficult conversations to be had; it allowed for the slow dawning of impossibly hard realities. There is also an ethical imperative for professionals towards the older person, perhaps, to allow him or her the opportunity to give consideration to the best way to experience any remaining time. This is not to say that older people are written off as hopeless cases, but if there are serious health concerns there is a tension that exists between an experience of quality or a time beset with further struggle, and exhaustion. In Mum's case, the medical team was seemingly right to offer her a moment's pause: will treatment extend her life or simply prolong her death (Jones and McCullough, 2014)?

With high-technology medical interventions there is a cost: for some, suffering continues in the name of life, any thought of dying obfuscated, and families do not feel ready to say goodbye. The play *Homeward Bound* (2016), written by Brian Daniels and developed by the National Council for Palliative Care, about Lesley Goodburn and her husband Seth, who died following a short struggle with pancreatic cancer, highlights this conflict between keeping people alive in hospital and the wishes of some patients to be given the opportunity to die peacefully at home.

Death can be seen as a failure of medicine, as if our finitude is nothing more than an existential change that can be rewritten, re-scripted, with appropriate technological intervention. For others, there is an understanding that medicine, for those who are terminally ill, is not about managing failure but rather about the alleviation of suffering, through the treatment of all forms of human pain.

> *I have learned from my life in medicine that death is not always an enemy. Often it is good medical treatment. Often it achieves what medicine cannot achieve— it stops suffering.*
>
> **CHRISTIAAN BARNARD (1980),**
> **GOOD LIFE, GOOD DEATH**

In line with a more stoic approach, Mum was given time. At least to explore her options. She was at a crossroads – in an in-between space between living and dying. In retrospect, the next moves that she took were a reflection of the way that she started to live in the gap.

On her return home from the specialist hospital, Mum immediately engaged with local palliative care services, despite some insistence that she was not quite dying yet; at the same time she had made the decision to receive any treatment possibilities open to her. So towards the end of January, a month to the day of the original seizure, mum had the biopsy while simultaneously being supported by the local palliative care team. That said, receiving the biopsy, though a relief to us all, was not without its considerable challenges.

Hospitals are under such huge pressure and, despite Mum receiving care at a centre of excellence, attempting to make sense of the systems, developing enough resilience to cope with the waits, is arguably too much pressure for a dying person. There is a constant fear, I imagine, that one is falling through the cracks, that you are not being kept in mind, that you must become the one who shouts the loudest to be heard. Clients with whom I work often talk of the complexity and confusion that their treatment evokes, yearning for something more simple where only one or two named practitioners are able to join up the dots on their behalf, a sense of a relationship, of knowing who is keeping you in mind.

This is not the fault of staff teams, but of a system that is being eroded systematically by the government, that is tired and under-resourced. Writing in August 2019, the independent think tank, The King's Fund, writes:

> After the most sustained funding squeeze in its history, the five-year funding deal for the NHS provides welcome relief and is generous compared to settlements for other public services. However, this deal does not extend to important areas of health spending, such as investment in buildings and equipment and training for staff, and leaves the NHS short of the resources it needs to both restore performance against key waiting times standards and transform services to deliver better care.

The days leading up to the biopsy, and the eventual day that Mum was invited into the hospital to have surgery, were characterised by intense anxiety. Though the hands-on care Mum received was without fail humane, the steps taken to gain entry into this unfamiliar site of care were nothing short of bewildering.

It compounded a confusion that was already becoming more pronounced as the glioblastoma reached further into her brain. Dad, too, shattered by the 24-hour care he was now giving Mum, found it hard to make sense of the process, which became increasingly shambolic on the day, of gaining access to a bed.

Mum had been told by the waiting list co-ordinator to call into the neuroscience ward on Wednesday, midday, to see if any beds were available. All of the existential uncertainty that she was managing, each moment, each day, was now being exacerbated by the structural uncertainties of the hospital; an absence of a containing organisational function at work (Armstrong, 2005), we might imagine. Mum had dutifully turned up, always early, a residual battle with impatience, but no beds were available.

Mum and Dad had arrived before 3pm, sitting alongside others in similar positions in the waiting room. For my father this would have been interminable. It is one of his long-time traits that his leg begins to judder when he feels the need to leave any situation, from a splash-out meal in a decent restaurant to an off-the-cuff visit to his grandchildren. A mollusc, my mother has always called him, a creature of his own well-constructed, routine wombspace. Mum would have noticed the shaking movement in his leg, and, as it would undoubtedly have unnerved her, she would have told him to leave; his anxiety communicating perhaps and disturbing an equilibrium she might have been working hard to sustain. But this is speculation since I was not there...

Despite the knowledge of her tumour, though, Mum was hiding the extent of her illness well. She was always well dressed, mascara on, handbag draped around her arm. To all intents and purposes, she was the picture of a plump but rather sophisticated older woman; and this is an image she had carefully put together throughout the entirety of her life. Given her roots in poverty, the presentation of elegance and an outward dignity had been vital to her.

Many people, perhaps Dad included, on that afternoon, at least, may not have realised the extent of damage going on beneath her skull. Dad left, sensing that his wife could handle the wait better than him, which temperamentally she could. She would be all right, she had convinced him and possibly herself. In the time that he left her to come to our home, given that it was closer than the journey back to the cottage, Mum – and her tumour – was sent for another MRI and she was moved from one room to another, having discussions with various doctors all alone, speech we might imagine becoming more garbled and incomprehensible. She was asked on several occasions what her name was, the year and the name of the hospital. We might not be hard pushed to understand that, tiring of all the questions, the wait, the movement in and out of rooms and scanning devices, with faltering mobility, that eventually she became exhausted; that she was more aware than ever of her failings and her diminished mental capacity. It was another family – sisters with a brother who was being treated for a glioblastoma – that rescued her, taking her to the room that had come available (a private one with ensuite bathroom facilities, with which she was delighted) finally at 7pm.

On learning that Mum was alone, in this bewilderment, I had charged to the hospital – furious but attempting, clumsily, to contain my anger – having just dropped my daughter back from a drama club. I wept as I drove; the idea of Mum abandoned there without familiar support was unbearable. Dad was a little shocked by my response and defensive, and somehow I understood in that instance that parents become older and older and older, and more and more vulnerable, until they die.

As I drove out of the house, Mum called me, insisting that no one should visit her that evening. But I was already on the way. Walking into her room, I found her there, already in her bedclothes, simply over the moon to see me. Mum broke into tears, drew me close and we cuddled, hard to know who was comforting whom. The distress of an afternoon waiting, alone and dependent on an unknown family who had their own glioblastoma with them, had taken its toll. At least I could be a reference point, a known quantity, a reminder for Mum that she was indeed Joyce Margaret Jones.

A nurse entered the room, as we sat close together, and repeated the battery of identifying questions all over again. Mum gave the nurse her name, *born 1940, now living in 2019, and this is my daughter.* Despite her insistence on the phone to the contrary, on one level Mum had needed some mothering; she needed me to shield her and to protect her from her own sense of diminishment. Yet on another, she had needed to demonstrate that she too was a mother – she told the nurse what I was doing, all the things that she was proud of, and so, in that moment, my imagined and real accomplishments became her own. A proud mother, rejoicing in the minor successes of her child, a sort of vicarious feedback loop. In that moment, she was not a woman with a brain tumour, feeling defeated and unseen, but someone who by proxy was still functioning and rejoicing and responsible.

'My lovely little daughter is here,' she had shouted as I entered the room. She was able to talk to me openly about her anxiety as she got moved around the rooms, how she had tried to shuffle along with her bags, putting too much weight on her arms and pulling her down, crouched; how the three sisters of the man with the GBM had kept her company and acted as navigators for her and their brother; how some members of staff were so accommodating but one or two others were not as sensitive to the problems she was having with her oversized bags and her oversized inflamed brain. She cried, 'What a stupid old woman.' We talked about how hard it was to ask for help, and she acknowledged that she had thought she was stronger than she was. She said that she knew I was robust enough to be there with her in this distressing moment. Inside I had wanted to cry while at the same time feeling so privileged that this big, sturdy woman trusted me enough to share this most shameful (for her) vulnerability.

As a small girl my mother had learned how to be resilient, and to look after herself. On many occasions she had had to stand up for herself against her older siblings, against her father, drunken and violent. In adulthood she had allowed herself to come to trust my father, and all this suppressed dependency of childhood – particularly in her later years – had found a reliable other to whom she could express it. She had learned to relax into his care, sometimes too much so, yet on this day – perhaps out of fear as much as anything and her desire to protect Dad from his own anxiety – she had pushed his care away. So it was that this awful moment had allowed me to become the bearer of her distress, and daughter simultaneously.

The nurse who had entered to check Mum's pulse and heart was beautiful, her skin like silk. Mum had told her so. She had always been someone to notice beauty, the aesthetic, and the tumour so far had not prevented this. She whispered to my mum that she had given the questions a good shot. We talked about it not being a test, 'I feel so stupid,' Mum said. The nurse told her that she had a tumour that was affecting her recall, but that she was not stupid. As we already knew, the tumour was causing expressive dyphasia and, though there were wobbly moments, her capacity, as defined by the Mental

Capacity Act (2005), to understand and process information, to make her own decisions, was not yet in question. Instead of concentrating on the answers *per se*, this nurse, with her thick accent – from another continent, I surmised – attuned to the undertones of distress, told Mum that she had an amazing smile and seemed like such a kind lady. With that, Mum seemed to regain some sense of balance, of self-belief; it is the understanding of others, the way we are seen, that can bring about a re-centring experience when we find ourselves in chaos. A reminder that, even in the worst of moments, we are all right. We are not in isolation, and while we might like to believe that we must retain our strength individually sometimes a gentle comment, interspersed with a containing presence or explanation, an-Other's capacity to notice the continued good while also recognising the struggle, is an invaluable communication that prompts a return to some form of solidity. 'In love,' Mum turned to me, 'all of this, Esther, in love.'

———————

The next day Mum was transferred to a neurology ward, and there she waited for the biopsy. If brain tumours are the primary site of the cancer and, if they are in an area of the brain which can be operated on, a small sample of the tissue may be taken to aid the diagnosis of the tumour type. Usually a biopsy is an operation that takes several hours and any possible risks will be explained to patients by the neurosurgeon. Sometimes and, if possible, a resection (surgical removal) of the whole tumour – or as much as possible – might take place. When only a part of the tumour is removed, surgeons call this debunking. Mum had been warned that this was not going to be possible for her. With a heart arrhythmia and high blood pressure, she had been on Warfarin, a blood-thinning agent, for over two years and sometimes it was a real, breathless struggle for her to walk for any distance.

Before the tumour had interrupted her life so dramatically, I had asked her to get second opinions on her breathlessness, fearing that she might simply collapse under the strain of trying to get her breath. Retrospectively, of course, we start to make links and to notice anxieties that were beneath the surface but not yet fully formed or which we might have partially chosen to ignore. We start to piece together all those incidents which, from the present moment, with a turned head, now look like red flags, signs that some sort of unravelling was already on the cards. Psychotherapists working with bereaved people often hear family members or spouses talk about the beginnings of the end, which were brushed to one side. Some people, perhaps those with formerly ambivalent feelings towards the parents or husbands, wives, who have died, pick up those red flags and whip themselves again and again in guilt: *they should have noticed sooner; A or B or C or D would still be alive now; if only I'd put more pressure on him to get checked, I knew it was bad but I didn't say.*

I wondered too if this breathlessness, now, was not so much Mum's heart but a tumour somehow starving her of oxygen – another mental tussle that has no basis in medical reality. What we all knew with certainty was that a resection would lead to a possibility of post-operative paralysis, but more importantly – given Mum's physical ill-health – it would be likely that her recovery would be too slow. Glioblastomas are notorious in growing back speedily and before she had recuperated it was likely that a resected tumour would be rebirthing itself like some kind of rabid alien.

This was a prompt to think about life, and to reflect upon quality of life – what does it look like to a woman of seventy-eight? Is it about struggle, invasive surgery, recovery –

slow and debilitating, increased dependency – only to die soon afterwards? Or about a pressure-free existence when you slow down according to your own bodily rhythm? The consultant had not taken a resection off the table, but it would have meant a report from an anaesthetist and further delay on treatment, and a tense uphill (or arguably downhill) struggle. Reading between the lines, as one sometimes has to do so, Mum had made the decision to compromise – hence the biopsy. She could have the surgery awake, and at least get to know once and for all what we were all faced with. It was as if, despite the threat to her own capacity to name things, this tumour had to be named.

Following any biopsy or surgery, cells from the tumour are analysed by a neuropathologist and this can take up to a week before a patient is called back to the neurosurgeon for confirmation. A neuropathologist examines the tumour for particular patterns of cells, cells which are characteristic of a variety of brain tumour-types and their gradings (from 1 to 4). This is not an easy process because some low grade and high grade brain tumours sometimes look very similar, nature's mimicry. Accurate diagnosis is of course important for all of those patients who are considering treatment because this will ascertain what the options are, and may be inclusive of possible clinical trials. With a diagnosis, we might imagine that we are more in control. This seemed to be my mother's thinking: somehow she would know how this tumour of hers would behave; how she might be able to keep it at bay – all being well with radiotherapy or chemotherapy; how, by giving it a name, the flow of information would help us to frame our experience and make sense of the storm in her brain. Perhaps sometimes these things help; of course they do: I have seen how knowledge curiously gives some people a sense of respite, as if, in knowing, a sense of control follows. For those who are struggling with the uncertainties of living with life-limiting conditions, the process of giving name to the experience can at least momentarily diminish the anguish before symptoms flare up again. Mostly, though, the respite is temporary and anxieties arise at different stages in the trajectory of dying.

> He tells me that he needs to know his wife's prognosis, but she has never asked the consultant. In fact she never asks for help, even when the pain in her side is unbearable. She will accept help but won't ask for it. How hard it is to reveal to ourselves our own weaknesses. He links his wife up with the Macmillan nurse and, as they leave the consultant's room, he does an about turn. 'Tell me,' he says, 'with the spread of the cancer to her spine, another hit, how long do you think she has this time?' His question is about managing his own uncertainty, on the one hand, but, breaking down, he also acknowledges that he is struggling to bear with the deadening effect of all these appointments, and the image of decline he sees each day, on his own formerly active life. These are undoubtedly the hardest, guiltiest feelings to admit.

Though Mum wanted to know, to know everything she could, there is something to be said for not knowing. Some clients I have avoid asking all the questions, and live through their illnesses – receiving treatment and understanding what the condition is – without overthinking the implications of decline, or planning for death. They seem to feel their way through things, alert and in attention to their own bodies. Some are lucky enough to book holiday after holiday after holiday, to celebrate birthday after birthday and enjoy the seasons as they unfold each year. They avoid consciously facing death head on, in language, yet seem connected to the rhythms of their own bodies, slowing down when they need to and ramping it up when the energy serves. In a sense they surrender, a sort of reverse process to a spontaneous home birth with minimal scans, minimal intervention. Sometimes I wonder about this curiously embodied way of dealing with physical illness and I understand why spouses need to know, more formally, than a dying person may need to: after all, perhaps she or he, quite simply, inhabits the bodyspace as a pregnant mother does.

The medicalisation of dying and death means, to an extent, that we are given insights into trajectories of illness that we would never once have known. Like birth, there were once times when a pregnant mother would not have been aware of the minute changes in her foetus, the hearing of the heartbeat, the size and length of his or her small body; there would have been a reliance on a sort of maternal instinct able to read the cues of the foetus. Of course, in those times, we would have experienced more maternal and neonatal deaths, but it is possible that we have moved pendulum-like to this highly controlled medicalised place. We live in rational times, with rational processes, and yet birth like death is never necessarily a tidy one which we are able to plan and manage. Nonetheless, for my mother she wanted to place her trust somewhere and, though I wondered about her continued desire to have a biopsy, she firmly believed in the authority of the medical model, not to save her but to at least guide her for now.

Following a biopsy there is a possibility that the tumour cells can be sent for 'biomarker testing', where changes in certain genes may indicate that some treatments might be more advantageous than others. Biomarkers may also be helpful in predicting the speed of tumour growth. The idea is that the bio marking of tumours is able to feed into research focused on improving survival and quality of life for people living and dying with brain tumours.

When the nurse specialist mentioned the possibility of bio marking to Mum, she seemed to relish the idea, the idea that the 'silly thing' could be used to advance medical research. She nodded her head and stated firmly, as if she were ordering from her favourite menu, 'I would like that.'

There was a naivety – and also strange omnipotence – about Mum, that somehow her tumour could leave its impact, that her life would have some sort of meaning in the domain of brain tumour research. Yet currently there is no centralised tissue bank to store samples of bio marking: according to the Brain Tumour Charity, this will need to meet with ethical approval under the Human Tissue Act.

On the ward, as Mum waited for a sign that her biopsy was to be scheduled, she had started to strike up conversations with people. She had noticed the woman opposite, who somehow held herself physically as if life had been too heavy, weighted her down, a woman churning inside and out. All the phone calls the woman made from her bed were loud, always furiously pressing numbers on her mobile phone. Mum had learned that her child was on the pupil premium, that the credit for the electricity was running low as she waited on the ward, that the social worker was trying her best but somehow failing to assist. The woman cursed, she raged, she hated, her thin body twisted and deprived. This was going on each day as Mum waited for several days on end, her turn to be seen being bumped by emergency admissions in need of immediate neurosurgery: car crashes, cyclists knocked down, drownings, beatings – you imagined it all.

Somehow the woman opposite, C, began to soften with Mum. Sitting there each day, Mum couldn't help but develop a language of community and common humanity: she took risks with love, offering it whenever she could. She was not the only one; people have this uncanny knack of reaching out to one another and establishing connection in bleak circumstances. This was not a new behaviour of Mum's, but somehow it became more urgent, more pronounced in those days on the ward. There was an outward push towards love, as if this manner of interaction was now the only one available to her.

'If I could come over to you,' she had said to the woman opposite, whose trauma emerged in bodily ticks and attacking sequences of words, '*I would cuddle you.*' Something in the naivety of Mum's approach seemed to defuse all the loathing and rage.

Several days went past; each morning Mum was ready for the biopsy: nil by mouth signs went up; the hospital gown on, back split for easy access; dvt stockings; legs being pumped at night to alleviate the growing signs of oedema. Mum was patient but the daily wait was beginning to take its toll. Dad stayed at our house, unsettled by the change to his routine. Soon Mum started to become defeated by the wait: there were small cracks appearing, small signs that she was beginning to feel as if her life had perhaps less value than a younger, healthier body. 'Perhaps they realise that there is nothing they can do?' she asked. Though she felt cared for by the nurses, who were busy but seemingly never busy enough to avoid contact with their patients, and at times talked to them about their work, her own day, the lack of movement, or progress towards the biopsy, began to play on her mind.

Being in a bay opposite C, though, meant that Mum was not able to indulge these thoughts of her own need for too long. One morning, as a nurse brought in a coffee for one of the weaker ladies, C became maddened, sensing that she was the rejected troublesome woman on the ward, the scapegoat, the pariah. 'Racist,' she shouted out of nowhere. 'I'm excluded in my community, excluded here, too.' Mum watched, quietly, as did my father and I. The nurse went forward, trying to calm C and asking her to explain. We might imagine that C had pushed people to their limits all her life, projecting her own fear of abandonment and rejection until they walked away and left her. We don't know what racist abuse she had endured, or what violations her body – malformed with MS – had undergone. The nurse was firm, boundaried, but not uncaring, and as she left C in a calmer frame of mind Mum could see her tears rise.

There is pain on hospital wards, and it leaks and finds itself in different places. Brutalised people often brutalise in turn, and someone ends up a receptacle for all those earlier wounds and attacks. Mum spoke to C from across the bed and peace began to descend. When the nurse returned Mum spoke to her too. These common threads of humanity: women and men simply trying to muddle along through the corridors of their own grief and heartache. Unlike a couple a few beds down who were shaking their heads, and understandably critical, Mum seemed to be able to encounter it without making judgement. This was, at least, where dying was taking her.

The stockings for her legs were agonising but she barely complained; the biopsy was cancelled again, and she remained stoic but concerned. I wondered if there was a sense of safety in the hospital; a relief of not burdening my father or me with worries. She was after all in good hands. This perhaps explained why she was not more forceful about the speed of the biopsy, though Dad and I behind the scenes were asking questions about its timings, a sense that – despite her relative acceptance of the situation – too much waiting can feel like a death in itself.

Soon Mum had befriended another woman on the ward, a Spanish woman interested in poetry and the arts. For two days they had talked about literature, and Mum had shared her love of Louis MacNeice's 'Sunlight on the Garden', reciting as much as she could. On the day Mum finally had her biopsy, I went into the hospital to the ward Mum had been in. She had gone into surgery, and she wouldn't be returning to that particular space with the lilac and light green curtaining again. C noticed me, and called out, explaining that Mum would go into a different ward on return from the biopsy. C had a friend with her, and her son too. The friend was braiding her hair, and adding extensions into the mix: she looked a little better. What a difference a bit of personal care can do; a sign of family and belonging.

She asks me how old Mum is, and I tell her. 'She's not like a seventy-eight-year-old, your mum. So, so lively. She has been so kind to me,' she says.

I ask her how she is, 'Headaches but that's nothing. Nothing compared to your Mum. Hope you find her. Give her my love,' she says. And it's funny how love begets love, even from those who appear so angry, so hardened by what life has thrown at them. I thought about Mum's impact in what would be the last weeks of her life, and how we can touch people at any point in our lives, leaving something good behind.

Jack Kornfield, the Buddhist psychotherapist, recently quoted the words of poet Ellen Basque, 'What if you knew you'd be the last to touch someone?' These words resonate not just with the work of those of us in palliative care, who often are quite literally the last to touch someone, but with us all in our encounters with one another. With the certainty of our endings in mind, perhaps there is no more salutary lesson than the one offered to us by the many people who are dying, that is to live and leave with love.

While it is the case that our spheres of influence are often minimal, we do all influence and make an impact on each other. Human beings are of course subject to nature's movements, to fleeting moments of serendipity or chance, yet we are also awake, with conscience and, most vitally, agential. We make choices based on what we encounter and how we interpret things. Those choices may appear small – 'I will choose to say thank you to the person who offers me a seat'; 'I will make sure that I show I am sorry when I need to be so; to say goodbye to those I leave' and so forth – or more impactful on a wider socio-political scale, or in the arts. What my mother was seemingly doing was choosing her endings wisely, playing them out with as much human kindness as she could possibly muster as she faced her own demise. And somehow I found this both as it should be and extraordinary at the same time.

Eventually, a few loops of the corridors later, I found Mum's new place in the hospital. I sat waiting in the ward for her return – no bed in the bay that Mum was due to be in. A strange, unfamiliar sense of panic engulfed me and, in that quiet space of waiting, tears surfaced as I thought about the emptiness that would soon be part of our lives; this bay with nothing in it, a symbol of Mum's impending absence. Soon that unwanted pause for reflection was interrupted.

'You are her daughter…,' a petite woman, with long auburn hair, and an uneven walk, spoke to me. She was serious, concerned, and I could see how difficult it must have been for her to find this spot, the asymmetry in her bodily movement, the wobbliness, somehow discordant with the zealousness of her mission to find Mum. 'I do not want to leave until I know she is all right and has not lost her speech, not her.' She continued, almost as if a speech had been prepared. 'She is such an amazing lady, and so very proud of you.' This woman whom I later discovered was from Spain – and now moved to a recovery ward, following her own neurosurgery – had returned to see that Mum and Mum's speech had survived the biopsy. Her concern was touching, as was her openness. She would return, she said, but as she shuffled around the corridor the deep breath, which I had taken in to hold back tears as I listened to her, was released. Hearing a stranger talk about my mother in this way, about my own mother's pride in me, seemed to confirm my fears about the woman I was soon to lose.

Mum, human to a fault, was far from perfect but at base she had often tried to be kind and giving. In my lifetime she had been a volatile ball of love, honesty and sometimes wild anger, her care for others linked to a raging fury about injustice, so aware she had been of what it was like for those who had never received any. She had perhaps spent so much of her energy repairing the wounds of her own childhood through her care of others that the splitting off of her own vulnerability poured into him or her or them. It did not go unnoticed that, having a glioblastoma – this angry explosive cancer that perhaps mimicked something of who she was – wreaking damage to her temporal lobe, the division between kindness and rage continued but that the tumour itself had absorbed all that fiery ardour, freeing Mum up, to an extent, to inhabit more fully the soft spirit that had co-existed alongside that harder volatile shell.

The nurse, one I had met back in January, during Mum's first stint in hospital, recognised me and recognised my tears. She puts her hand on my shoulders and blesses me. It is nothing special, no deep listening, no sophisticated processing, but it is what any human needs when they are holding on to pain, trying not to let it out. It is that acknowledging touch and nod of the head that says it is all right, and we understand. The tears slowly graced my cheeks and it, and I, was all right again.

A woman to the right asks me who I am waiting for and we begin talking about the hospital: she is full of admiration. She tells me that Mum will be fixed here, that she's been fixed there following a life-threatening aneurysm. She's only just survived, and she begins running through all the names of all the nurses and doctors who have helped her. Hers is the gratitude of someone who has come so close to death, and survived; she notes each person and retains information about them. Each doctor and nurse that has given her life value, in turn she gives value to them; a reciprocity of recognition that perhaps the staff will never hear about.

Moments passed, and then I heard her voice, a little distance away, from the corridor. Mum is laughing, unexpected, so awake after the drilling in her skull, a surgeon and his team fishing those twisting, turning tentacles out. The recovery nurse is pushing Mum and chatting at the same time: it's a conversation about Brexit, both are bemoaning its already divisive effect on human relations. The nurse looks at me, a backpack she carries with emergency supplies post-op. 'She's been great, she hasn't stopped talking.' Mum tells me later that the surgeon had to ask her to be quiet for a little while. Sometimes I wonder if Mum's chatter covers her nerves, but she says nothing – ever – about fear. Sadness, but never fear.

Mum and I sit together. I am so glad to be with her following her biopsy. She tells me what she remembers, some bright lights on a screen, and some, it seems, in her mind. I think of clients who have had near-death experiences and how they talk of lights, blue and white lights, the pull into some out-there-mos-phere that belongs to spirits and angels. I wonder if Mum feels she has been touched by something beyond the technical confines of the operating room. She remembers the sensation of something wiry digging into her head, which counters my own flight to an oceanic weightless place, and what feels like the pull of a wormlike strand deeply embedded in her head – some part of the tumour, we might imagine. Mum says that she is alright, and I believe her. She is starving hungry though, the one thing on her mind sandwiches and hot chocolate, Mum ever the more grounded member of our family. Soon the nurses – a pair – come in, they remember Mum from January and are delighted to have her back. It's incredible that she is remembered, and I can see that she feels like a someone, a real person, cared for and liked. These small recognitions are vital to the sustenance of life and of self. We are lucky, with this NHS. And I am lucky to be with her, in these role-reversing times. Daughters to mothers, mothers to daughters, and back again, so familiar these stories are to me:

> The woman comes for her second session. The week before, the first after her mother has died, she was overwhelmed, sobbing, broken in the aftermath of her mother's death, just two days before. This week she is different, dressed in a furry, cosy jumper, earrings now on, a little mascara. She isn't crying, yet she is deeply sad, able to consider her own pain. But, today, she talks about an absence of regret. 'I was there, with her, all the way along.' Tears well up in her eyes. 'It was manic, intense, the day they suddenly realised that there was nothing left they could do for her. I was there with Mum, I could see the shocked expression on her face, the realisation that there might only be a couple of days left. But at least I was there, in the room with her, and then in the car and I have been at the appointments and by her bedside as she

ebbed away.' She sighs. We talk about her exhaustion,
the relentlessness of her Mum's precariousness and the
responsibility of ongoing care, but she knows somehow
that – in the midst of this searing pain – she will endure
and be all right. 'Because I have no regrets.'

Before the hot chocolate comes, I nip to the café in the
hospital in case there is a wait and Mum begins to become dry
of mouth. I nip to the café, too, as I now know Mum is still
alive, despite all my unconscious fears of absence – I nip to the
café to have a break from the thoughts and to be able to make
simple easy choices about milk or sugar, orange juice or apple,
to see a cashier and to smile, make a light joke about working
late. I nip to the café to return to an old normal, to replace this
new normal of hospitals, and spindly tumorous chords, speech
loss and a mum's deterioration.

As I turn out of the neuroscience wards, a man is coming
in, walking slowly, clutching his back; he is young. We share
a minute in conversation and he tells me he has had part of
his spine removed, a spinal-blastoma. I wish him well with his
recovery, and I hope he will live for a long time. Again, this
kindness, about him, that does not go unnoticed. Despite his
own experience, his own threatened mortality, he asks about
my mum. It all seems so easy, doesn't it, to enquire about others
even when we are ill and damaged ourselves, and yet it must
take effort… but these moments of touch and opening out are
all around in the hospital between unwell patients, between
family visitors and staff; there is a strange compassionate fabric
– imperfect, sometimes awkward and clumsy – of human
interaction. I cannot cease to be moved by it all. In hospice
settings, similar formations play out among those living with
terminal illness who form communities among them, looking

out for, supporting one another until life cannot give any more. Of course it is not always rosy, and in among such groups there will sometimes be voices of dissent, or the odd scapegoat may be found, or another member finds themselves under envious attack for taking up more space with staff and volunteers than others, but in general these groups with rather problematic titles, such as well-being days, are supportive and respectful.

DYING PLANS: STOICS

*'Watching a peaceful death of a human being
reminds us of a falling star; one of a million
lights in a vast sky that flares up for a brief
moment only to disappear into the endless night
forever. To be a therapist to a dying patient
makes us aware of the uniqueness of each
individual in this vast sea of humanity.'*

Elisabeth Kubler-Ross (1969)

T he well-known chaplain, Peter Speck, once suggested
that the exhaustion of staff in palliative care resulted
from a pressure of having to uphold the fantasy of
'chronic niceness' in daily encounters (O'Mahony et al, 2019).
It was as if palliative care professionals had idealised the work,
the care, idealised what death and dying can bring to us –
those living with terminal illnesses and those living without
– and disavowed the difficulties, the tensions among families

and patients and doctors, failed to give the hardships, the awfulness, thought.

Yet there is mess and disturbance in the corridors of palliative care as there are in any organisations that focus on the human. The human condition itself is never tidy, and easily categorised forms that we fill can never encapsulate the crazed and crazy undertones of our collective experience. However, what might just happen when we are faced with death and decline on a daily basis is that there is a greater commitment in fact to trying, sometimes gauchely, to talk, to think, to reflect on these unavoidable uglier realities. Not always, but often, people have the pressing need to discover truths about themselves, and about others; the small talk exists of course – the preoccupation with hair-dos or matching cushions continues, the chat about sweet cakes and tea that go so far to cover up – yet they find an easier place at times next to conversations about existential fears, about confusing wants, needs for meaning and intimacy and relatedness. When we step into the mess, perhaps we are also given the opportunity to notice the beauty too. I would tend to agree with Rachel Clarke, palliative care doctor and author of *Dear Life,* who writes in the *Guardian* (January 2020) about NHS hospice work, 'All that is good in human nature – courage, compassion, our capacity to love – is here in its most distilled form.' But of course, as Speck's point might suggest, the mess must be given equal coverage to the beauty.

By the time I return to the ward, the man serving hot drinks is by Mum's bed. They share a quick joke about how hot the hot chocolate is, and then he departs. For some reason, Mum is remembering her confirmation as an eleven-year-old and the white dress her mother sewed by hand. I find myself back with the airy feeling of angels, momentarily, and outer body experiences. My grandmother had made the dress with bed linen. Mum remembers having complained to her mother, and the next day my grandmother had gone out to purchase a silky taffeta material, staying up all night again sewing. I think about fairy tales, the elves and the shoemaker, and I am glad that in among the harder, harsher, violent memories that Mum has of childhood there are countering memories of a generous, patient mother. But like all memories and experiences, there is nuance there and soon Mum opens up more honestly. She talks about how ashamed she was of her mother, who continued to read romantic magazines when she had begun to read Shakespeare and Milton. She remembers the distance that began to open up and, even now, at seventy-eight, guilt underpins the fragments of these stories. What damage do we do to our mothers? What damage had I done to mine when I rejected her guidance as an adolescent, her ideas of what I was to become? And yet here I am hearing and taking in her histories, the handing down of mothers' stories reshaped, rewritten. What would we be if we hadn't rejected our mothers whom one day – if lucky – we might also find a way back to in order to say one final goodbye? I think about the way that my mother grieved the death of her own mother, and the way she in fact slipped into a state of mind akin to Freud's melancholia, how she started to morph into my grandmother, more silent, less mobile, growing in bodyweight, developing a late-onset sweet, sweet tooth. I wondered about Mum's ambivalence towards her mother, the better idealised object in what might be considered a destructive parental partnership, and how all the ill feeling went underground, turned inwards, a punishing castigating voice, when my grandmother died. It all makes sense now.

Freud (2017) makes this link clear:

[M]elancholia contains something more than a normal mourning. In melancholia the relation to the object is no simple one; it is complicated by the conflict due to ambivalence... countless separate struggles are carried on over the object, in which hate and love contend with each other. (p.256)

For Freud, melancholia 'behaves like an open wound' (1917, p. 253), and the aggressive feelings that the survivor has towards the dead person are collected and subsequently used in the service of a persistent self-recriminatory attack (Green 2013); it is the relentless attachment to the ambivalence towards the lost object that gives the grieving a sense of paralysis and stuckness. My mother's grieving following the death of her own mother took on this quality, so much had she wished to protect and sanctify the memory of her mother – as perhaps she had done in childhood. It is possible that this ongoing struggle to look after her mother from the raging barrage of her father, the strange symbiosis she had experienced as the child protector, meant that Mum had perhaps never fully resolved her psychic separation from her own mum. As Irving Leon (1999) writes:

Object relations theory views mourning as a painful recapitulation of early depressive fears of one's inner world being bereft, without the comforting presence of benevolent figures (Klein, 1940, p. 383).

The difficulty of separating from maternal figures was perhaps an ongoing transgenerational difficulty that was part of our family's history: my grandmother herself had had to force a radical separation from her own mother, marrying a man, lowly of class and education, that her own mother –

a shop owner of good repute – violently disapproved of; my separations, which were ongoing until my twenties, were also fraught and conflictual until the therapeutic couch helped me to make sense of my pressing and instinctual need to disentangle myself from Mum. And it is, as Benjamin (2006) argues, this movement towards separation and in-between space which allows for a more easy and comfortable proximity, in which two people with their own complex subjectivities are able to interrelate differentiated-yet-close, with greater respect and recognition. And so my mother, and many mothers, continue to be important figures in my life.

I think of all the different forms of mothers who have brought to life aspects of who I am – incisive powerful supervisors, minds overflowing with both nurture and intellectual, challenging sustenance; au pairs, creative and playful, surrogates; and my own mother – whose initially adhesive, narcissistic love gave way to something more real, more full and grounded. And, god, sometimes the gratitude itself hurts: for one day all these mothers will no longer be.

As she sits with her hot chocolate, cupped in her hands, she says, 'You must go home, Ess, to our children. Love, love, love.' She means this. In this moment, she becomes the Mother of all mothers, and of all children.

Mum does not stay in hospital long after the biopsy and two days later – after a day's observations – she returns home. I have visited each day, my work supportive, understanding, and I am there as she is discharged. Mum is delighted to return home, to the quiet familiarity of the cottage, and as a family we seem to be in good shape, holding out hopes for the next stage of treatment. For now, we fantasise that the biopsy will show that there has been a mistaken reading of the scans, that the tumour is something altogether more benign than a grade 4 glioblastoma, a simulacrum of the tentacled beast that has engulfed her temporal lobe. And yet I know rationally that, with the advancements in medical technology and fMRIs, this is so very unlikely. Whether I can call it hope, I am not sure, but what I wish for is that Mum may have at least a year of family life, in which she can continue to speak.

In the midst of these optimistic thoughts of treatment intervention and life-prolonging possibilities, there is the constant pull to the reality of death. Mum does not shy away from it. We sit down and, once again, she runs through her advance care plan verbally. She talks through all the treatments she will refuse – feeding pegs, resuscitation – and goes over her funeral. She will have a small family gathering under the mulberry tree in the garden – and now she brings my son and daughter by her in her chair, cuddling both of them close to her plump, fleshy chest. She tells them both that she wants to share out any of her jewellery with them. She apologises to my son, explaining she only has her brother's watches, who died at eighteen, ones which no longer work but which hold fading fragments of a past. I feel uneasy, as if the transference of these watches to my son will pass down a familial curse of youthful death, but I shake the thought from my mind. Not all sons and brothers perish.

My mother is clearing away, and handing down, a sort of living ceremony in which she enjoys seeing her treasures distributed among those she loves. I find her jewellery boxes and together – over an hour's activity – we talk about earrings, rings, bracelets that have been in her family, and on her wrists, for years. This awful moment of stripping away is nonetheless filled with laughter and storytelling and love. Our children look to Mum, and she looks to them. Neither of them fully grasp that this is an active communication of a woman who is relinquishing her hold on life, a symbolic act of giving-in-dying, and so they speak squarely about the garish earrings they can't stand, the bracelets that Mum should give to the charity shops; and Mum is not hurt that some jewels are rejected. Rather she seems to delight in their lack of self-consciousness, this freedom to be themselves, no airs, no graces, no clumsy politesse; no need to protect the grown-ups.

People who are dying often feel a tremendous relief in offering up what they have – both in terms of life's lessons as well as objects – to family members. This is a kind of tidying up and gifting before the final escape. Mum was overjoyed when her jewellery boxes had been cleared, with all but her bejewelled stalwarts left. 'Thank you,' she said. My mother's materialism had often irritated me, and I had spent a lifetime avoiding shopping expeditions and fancy clothes. As we sat together here over her collection, for the first time I sensed a greater tolerance of these pleasures she gave herself, embedded as they were in the narrative of material deprivation she had known so well. I walked around the cottage, noticing the myriad cups and saucers, the bookshelves brimming, the paintings hung, the shoes, the clothes – for a woman who had grown up in poverty, deprived at times of a roof over her head, it made sense that she had had to house herself in so many things. The material can understandably become an exoskeletal scaffolding to some, whose daily economic and housing uncertainties leave a constant nagging and frightening anxiety. And yet, in my father – through the relational – I believe she had found a more intimate sort of scaffolding that had brought about a greater internal security which meant, inversely, that she was now able to give it all away and that without these external

sources of structure she was in fact whole, full, no longer in
need, and stoic.

Eventually the ten-day wait to see the neurosurgeon was
over. After over an hour in the waiting room we were called
into a small room midway along the beige-walled corridor.
We had spent the hour observing the comings and goings: a
woman in a floral shirt, possibly the administrator, had paced
up and down the corridors so many times that you almost
hoped she'd had a Fitbit calculating her steps; a nursing assistant,
whose ill-conceived patter made you wonder if he had another
income stream as an entertainer at kids' parties; a young doctor,
catwalk-model looks, stopping, noting, disappearing; a man,
wheelchair-bound, who kept forcing himself up as if to walk;
a woman with a breathing tube forcing a smile; and a man who
abandoned his own appointment to take his mate for a knee
replacement in Solihull: the waiting room itself a patchwork
of lives and human stories.

'So do we know what it is?' Mum had asked, finally meeting
with the neurosurgeon and the neuro-specialist nurse with the
gentle demeanour. And so there it was: the biopsy confirmed
what we had known and simultaneously not wanted to know.
Mum definitively had a glioblastoma. She was asked questions
about how she was dealing with daily life. There might have
been an expectation that Mum would have responded with
some description of her activities of daily living, how she had
noticed the tumour's effects or not. But what she said was
staggering, representative of my terminal Mum. 'How am I
getting on?' she had said. 'With love, all of this with love. We
are receiving the most remarkable care.'

I see the nurse's face, the way she is touched, her care and
that of her colleague's care acknowledged. She is moved.
'You are too kind to us.' In these short exchanges, we could

all perhaps see what it meant to be fully human. Receiving love helps us learn how to love; work conducted on the developmental damage done to Romanian orphans who were left to cry it out in rooms filled with neglected children showed that there was a virtual black hole in the orbitofrontal cortex (Gerdhart, 2014), the site of the brain that develops empathy and sensitivity to others. We need love in order to cultivate it in ourselves and in others; the bedrock of connection, the sustenance of relationships. Despite her ever diminishing brain and cognitive ability, it was seemingly the case that there was no black hole of love for Mum; seemingly, this was more alive than ever.

Mum looked the part. She had on her favourite coat, her make-up, and perhaps steroids, adrenalin, and her residual awareness of the gaze of other people, all pushing her and her speech on. She was articulate, following almost everything the neurosurgeon was saying. 'You are doing well with your speech,' he said, Dad nodding in the corner, unconvinced, knowing that at home Mum was often garbled, her words slowed to a relative standstill when the steroids wore off. It was agreed that Mum's next meeting would be with an oncologist, one of the best in her field, a 'woman who doesn't give up', who was also running clinical trials for glioblastomas; treatment options would be discussed and a plan would be made. There was a sense of possibility in the room, and I wondered what our family had communicated to the professionals: a desire to ward off death, to live at all costs? Had he felt that he needed to sell us an optimistic line?

Nonetheless meetings with consultants often provide a sense of being held, on some level, for the patient and their families, even if nothing conclusive is arranged. The meetings often end with further meetings in view. In our case, the family would for another week be waiting to see what was next, what could work and when it would take place. Mum seemed to have inordinate trust in the professionals, able to tolerate the fact that we were coming away with nothing set in stone. We took her lead, yet secretly I wanted more, holding on to the hope that somehow perhaps she could be saved. 'I am going to do whatever it is,' she said, as if she could read my mind, 'that I can do for you, your father and the kids.' As a woman who had claimed she had lived a life that was good enough for her, Mum's desire to live was not about unfulfilled achievement or finding meaning, it was quite simply to spend time with those with whom she felt deeply connected.

A couple of weeks following the meeting with the neurosurgeon, I met Mum and Dad in a bustling café – which I barely paid attention to – at the new hospital's entrance. Here we were due to meet with the oncologist who would take over Mum's care and treatment options.

As we navigated this new hospital, I noticed that Mum was willing herself on, forcing herself to walk. Only a week had passed since I saw her, and now the struggle to move was more pronounced. Though I have seen this time and time again in the corridors of palliative care and in care homes that I have worked in; though with others I am able to slow my pace in order to be alongside, watching my own Mum's strength ebb away hurt. Her breathing was laboured, her face flush, the sheer weight of her tiredness, heavy muscles, heavy heart left my father and I helpless. Yet she would not give in, doggedly pushing on, stopping herself for momentary breaks against the wall, covered in brightly coloured images depicting well-being. Dad offers Mum a wheelchair, wanting to take the struggle away, but she refuses as if any act of disablement will give her permission to sink into death.

A husband recounts, in minute detail, how his wife will never accept his suggestion of help, but will sometimes agree to an easier alternative from a nurse. 'She is proud,' he says, 'and she doesn't want me to see her weaken.' He tells me about her childhood and about the way her father took up all the space in the home, that his needs took precedence, all others shadowlike and under his control. 'She always forgoes her own needs.' Even with the rapid progression of her illness, we might imagine, this internal father is telling her 'no'.

Once we get to the narrow corridor of the waiting room, Mum is relieved. She sits down and begins to close her eyes. This journey has tired her out, as has the cancer invading her brain. Somewhere deep inside, I have a sense that – despite the steroids which are managing to retain perhaps three-quarters of Mum's speech – this tumour of hers is marching on like Hannibal's troops crossing the rugged Alpine mountains. We might not be surprised that a woman with such stamina and ferocious determination would grow a tumour with similar qualities. Goldberg et al. (1981), psychotherapeutic practitioners working in the field of oncology, suggest that there may be causative links between the development of cancer and the emotional constitution of a patient. Relatedly, I often wondered if Mum's sometimes explosive temper – the way she must have held in anger, all too tightly, before it reached a crescendo – had put too much pressure on her brain.

In the waiting area, after a short rest, Mum had begun to open her eyes again, and was smiling rather intently at a woman without much hair. It seemed as if Mum was looking at her with a degree of sympathy, as she herself still had a full head of hair. Before long a conversation had struck up and it transpired the woman opposite, accompanied by her teenage daughter, was living with multiple brain tumours. She had undergone radiotherapy for several weeks, and thereafter the tumours had shrunk. Her life expectancy from diagnosis had been six months, but she had shot past this *dead*line by three months and was now living in her ninth month. I watched her daughter, smiling as her Mum told her story, and I wondered how she was managing.

'She is happy like me,' said Mum, watching this young daughter and mother together laughing and telling jokes. 'I have a brain tumour,' says the woman. 'What can I do?' as if she were explaining her need to laugh, as if she were saying *all I have now are my people and my humour.* Laughter is breaking out in the corridor, but this is no party. It is also a sombre place reserved for those who fear they might be dying. A consultant appears and tells them to quieten down: for all those who push away the pain in laughter there are others who are barely holding on to themselves.

A visit to a woman who had been struggling with intermittent brain tumours appearing and disappearing – with treatment – over many years was finally crumbling under the pressure of holding herself together in the face of the cumulative losses she had incurred. This last tumour was inoperable, defeating her. Each movement she made was painfully slow, her speech warped and elongated: tumours do strange things to speech and to time. In the room with her there was a uniquely curious mix of zen-like focus, a noticing, and also a silent anger that was paralysing. Strait-jacketed by the tumour, the suspension of time; how might she ever speak to this experience that was killing her? What possibility was there

for letting something out, the rage of her predicament
or any sense of hope that still existed in breath alone?

It is strange to think that we can find some hope in the thought that there might be an extension to life, of all but a few months, but when you are faced with dying or when someone you love is dying all time can become a gift before that time starts to take from you any sense of continuity and living.

Irving Leon (1999) writes:

Death shakes the cohesion of the self. The coherence of one's self-representation is initially based on the early sense of an intact body. Death cracks that coherence because the survivor has to confront the bodily disintegration of the deceased. Indirectly, bereavement foreshadows the vulnerability of our own bodies in the aging process and its inevitable decay after death. (p. 386)

And so time alongside the dying is both precious and painfully disruptive.

The oncologist is methodical, no-nonsense, professional. She wants to find cures. She discusses a new clinical trial, and the more realistic options for Mum. A Macmillan nurse lingers in the background, waiting for the moment to ask Mum what she wants to do – stoics or heroics. The oncologist begins to inhabit a humane space, she listens, she asks Mum who she is and what her life has been about.

We tell Mum that we want her to stay around as long as possible. This is the moment for the Macmillan nurse to step in: patients' wants and wishes, a voice heard, vital. 'I want to do my best to stay with all six of my family as long as possible in love.' It is, for Mum, all about the love, what sounds at times like a sentimental kind of oceanic floaty wombspace; but she knows that love also requires difficult conversations and honesty like never before.

The oncologist nods, also tough, a fighter. We had noticed that she herself had some kind of disability, a mobility problem curtailing her freedom of movement. We don't thank people enough. She guides us all through the treatment and what to expect: palliative radiotherapy is on offer until we know, from the biopsy, whether the tumour is chemo-responsive.

With radiotherapy, a mask will be made of Mum's face and head; there must be no head movement during treatment, the radiotherapy beams have to be specific, on point, directly onto the tumour site. Hair loss, asks Mum, a huge concern. And she is relieved to hear that the hair loss will only occur at the site. She cannot get much more tired, I fear, but with radiotherapy there will be more tiredness, possible skin rashes and subsequently creams to put it right. She will have the treatment at the original hospital – which Mum knows and likes. This is a relief to her.

Mum is given a consent form, and she expresses delight at being able to sign her name still. Skills she thought she'd lost. A coming back to herself through the written word, the identifying mark of a name.

We spend some time in the room, with Mum opening up, her insight into her situation striking. She talks about her speech going missing, the muddle of daily life, the curious temporal dissonance she is experiencing where time becomes suspended, as if nothing is moving on. The oncologist understands, it is the malfunction in her temporal lobe... They laugh together, '*Silent Witness*,' says Mum, 'It goes on for five hours.'

The oncologist's professional mask is far from rigid, and moves further into the human realm of the relational. She wants to know Mum, what makes her tick. She notes that Mum was once an English teacher, asks her about the plays she has put on, talks about poetry, song, foster care. 'If you are frustrated and can't get the words out, try singing them, it's a different part of the brain,' she says, cottoning on to the fact that music and song might be a way in to communication when retrieval and speech become too hard. 'Think of the thousands of people whose lives you will have touched,' she ends. Two women who, in all simplicity, will have touched many lives, a point of contact, patient and doctor.

Throughout all this time, it sounds as if my life as a mother and as a psychotherapist in palliative care were on hold. In real terms they were not; I was still going about my duties – school pick-up and drop-off, playing with the children, doing homework, backwards and forwards to activities, meeting clients, attending meetings, facilitating group supervision. For family members who are supporting a terminally ill person, life goes on around, and though on the surface everything continued as before – apart from the occasional meeting with the oncologist or neurosurgeon and the longer telephone calls – there was a constant fear of loss that underpinned the quotidian; the anticipation and recognition that the imagined future would be permanently changed.

Dad takes Mum for her appointment to have the radiotherapy mask fitted, and the cogs in the treatment wheel begin to start turning. A date is given for the initial sessions, and we are all set. We plan an early birthday celebration for my son, so that Mum can be there – because we are due to be on holiday on the actual date of his birthday. Mum offers him a gift of books, ones he can keep, and a wooden warrior toy to become part of the collection she has bought him since he was two. We know this will be the last set of birthday presents she is able to choose, and it is poignant. She bends down and watches him open them, enjoying every small moment of his surprise. But it tires her, our collective energy and possibly the profound realisation that every moment like this that she experiences has little likelihood of coming around again.

A planned skiing holiday with our family is on the horizon and I am torn. I try to tease apart where I will be most needed, and where I will rest most easily. My husband recognises how difficult such choices are, having helped his mother and father as much as he could have done when his own father was dying. Though I am anxious about being an absent mother if there were to be an accident – aware more than ever of life's fragilities – I also know they will be in safe hands with Matt. Having a partner or siblings, good friends, that have an understanding of the inner conflict that anticipatory grief can arouse is invaluable. In the end, what becomes more pressing is my fear that my Mum will die without me present and so I stay back. This theme of presence and absence will become a constant in our lives as we grieve.

We speak, Mum and I. As ever, still a mother, she tells me that I should take a rest and spend my time with the children. I relinquish my own authority, and do as I am told: this was the permission that I was looking for. All the while, anxiety is present. After all, Mum's first seizure had taken place just days before we were due to leave a different mountain range.

Mountains, vast and statuesque, an alternative landscape, so far from roads, aeroplanes, washing machines, routines, death; I had needed to escape. And on some days – though I am in contact with Mum – I try to pretend that she is doing well. Only the slight deterioration in one or two words reminds me that she isn't, but on the phone she is buoyant – protecting us again – about the treatment that will begin on our return.

For many parents, even in those moments where the roles

reverse and our children care for us, we continue to parent. Mum seemed so sure that she wanted me, and our family, to continue to live, to move about in the richness of our own experience, to err on the side of life. In all of her own personal wobbliness, it was as if she was nonetheless attempting to be a continual secure base (Bowlby, 1988).

The writing of Greengrass (2018), her exploration of what it was to become a mother, albeit a fictional one, resonated:

> It is a balance – to show enough love that she is sure of me but not so much that she stays close: the fact but not the size of it – and it is an effort, as I encourage her to disentangle herself from my gaze, to discard the aching want to have her back… (p. 125).

But we were not talking about a small child to a young mother, separating and individuating and reaching new developmental stages. Rather this disentangling was towards a final parting and the disentanglement of years of human connection, of arguments, of care, of concern and laughter. And so this was Mum's protection and preparation simultaneously, perhaps.

> Sometimes we hear of people in our work, patients who stop us in our tracks, a person who has made a huge impact on the staff team, a legacy of learning, who may at times begin to be sanctified, idealised in their dying. Psychotherapists might be suspicious, wondering where the negative countertransference lies, where has the nuance gone, yet sometimes people do meet with death with such an overwhelming generosity of spirit that it is hard to find the leaks of anger, anxiety, fear in them. One among many of such patients had a gaping hole in

his body, an abyss which he was staring down with his life. The wound needed dressing, it was frightening to see, the stench awful, yet those that cared for him were always able to go near him, with minimal anxiety, if any, because he had contained himself till the end. What people remember is his gratitude, his concern for others, his quiet concentration on what he still had in life. And though we might imagine that this was a man constantly working on his own containment, we might also see this as an act of giving in the final days of life. His death would not become a haunting.

Dad is anxious about the radiotherapy, about the three weeks of round trips to a hospital over an hour away: he anticipates the disorienting drives in the dark backwards and forwards. He agrees that I can take Mum for the middle week.

The first time Mum arrives for radiotherapy, she has difficulty consenting to the individual treatment: she cannot say her name or her date of birth; expressing these simple facts are impossible. As we wait for the go-ahead she is called away, asked to meet with a consultant. I imagine what she is thinking: a naughty girl unable to pass the test. 'Perhaps,' she says, 'they won't let me have it.' I cannot reassure her because I too do not know. Dad also follows; we have all been invited in: we have no idea. I ask the nurse we are following. She explains that this is to give Mum further results from the biopsy: momentary relief.

The oncologist is a young man, attentive to the affective flows between us all – patient, daughter, carer-husband. He tells Mum that her tumour is chemo-responsive: there are pros and cons; temozolomide might tire her further, she will keep her hair, it might aggressively stop the tumour cells from growing; but there can be sickness and nausea, a less efficient immune system, blood count depletion. Mum wants to take the chemo tablets. There is no travel time involved; they can be taken at home. She attempts to sign the consent form once again, but her signature is barely readable – so much change in so short a time; Dad countersigns. The tablets will be available after the radiotherapy: today will be a long day in the corridors of this giant, but efficient establishment. A strange sense of hope returns, the mention of chemotherapy – while debilitating – is synonymous with living with cancer. And yet it is clear that Mum is gradually succumbing to this 'bullish silly thing' of hers.

The following three weeks involve a daily drive to the hospital. In the second week, I become Mum's driver. We chat all the way to the hospital. She is preoccupied each time with practising her name over and over again, and then her date of birth. We write it down on a piece of paper that she shoves into her bag. She takes it out intermittently during the journey and tries to read the words in front of her. Her hit rate is low.

We take a cheese sandwich, a small one, and a few grapes. The same every day. The routine is helping: the familiarity provides a frame of reference in these bewildering times. When so much is unfamiliar – her own speech even, twists and turns of words that sound make-believe, a kind of babbling from someone in early childhood – the familiar becomes the anchorage of the everyday, a way of coping and navigating the continual flux. We stop each time at the café and have a hot chocolate together; we practise her name again. One day we sing her name over ten times in the car, as we had been advised by the oncologist; still it didn't quite stick. I see how dreadful it is for her to know herself and sense she is losing herself at the same time; yet she continues, because she has always continued. Once a survivor, always a survivor, she reminds me of other clients who take up life as if it is a battle – because, for them, it has been.

She is standing in her kitchen, sobbing. 'I am so cross with myself,' she says, 'I am letting myself down, because this is getting to me.' The woman has several illnesses, all collaborating, plotting, it seems, to put her life under threat. She has had this before, as a small child, where almost every adult gathered together abusively and narcissistically to break her and her siblings. She survived, she learned how to be robust, the eldest, and tried to become the good object she had never experienced; or imbibed. But now, she fears she can't survive this, and hates herself for asking for help, hates seeing all this stored-up need that is about to burst through the surface of her resilient carapace.

Mum could not bear to show that she too was struggling, could not bear that she was finding it hard to say her name. As we turned the corridors each day in the hospital, Mum now in a wheelchair, to the space-age-like room – pink lines forming a large square around the edges of the laminate floor, signs of DO NOT ENTER – where the radiotherapy took place, Mum would begin to prepare herself; her strategy to make light of the semantic losses, all that once exciting verbal dexterity. Could the radiographers see anything left of the woman she once was?

Waiting rooms for people with cancer are no different from any other waiting rooms: people are impatient, small talk is made, people knit, read books, moan, giggle, bring children, drop asleep. Yet one certainty exists: there are people in these rooms whose distance from death is closer than most, and so stories of survival and defeat abound. Owing to the sense that linear time was slowing down, Mum would ask every five to ten minutes what the time was. She felt that she had been waiting all her life. Cognitively she was unable to say that she was anxious, and seemed to smile through most of the wait, yet her relentless checking of the time also seemed anxious. She expressly denied this, and said quite simply that time was becoming more and more protracted like a giraffe's neck; a portal into stasis. A woman in the waiting room was knitting, reporting on her seventh cancer-free year. I could not summon up a sense of joy for her, my fears about my mother's prognosis perhaps getting in the way. But it was also the way that she was inhabiting the narrative of the fighter, the strong, combative cancer winner that bothered me: while she was smug in her survival, she positioned her husband – to the left of her – as weak, the man battling prostate cancer and not doing so well. We can all be guilty of these paranoid-schizoid splits, disavowals of our own vulnerabilities, the divisions into strong and weak, love and hate, well and ill, at different times in our lives, but here – just here – in the cancer room, I couldn't stomach it and wanted to turn on my heels, wheel Mum out of there and into the quiet safety of her cottage where she could just be without these trades of winning and losing, battles fought and won. How this language, I thought, of war does so much damage to the human psyche, to all of us simply trying to muddle along with whichever conditions befall us…

Mum-before-radiotherapy and Mum-after-radiotherapy were two different versions of the same woman. I wondered how much this was the treatment's impact, or the subsidence of pre-treatment anxiety. No longer focused on getting her name right, she began the long drive home speaking – free-flowing sentences that returned her to different parts of her past. Her language was full, articulate, minimally disrupted, and she was happy. Happy to be able to talk so well. She talked about her past, our family, my dad. She reminded me to eat as we raced up and down the motorway. She talked about the radiographers, the futuristic technical equipment, her 'lovely mask' which she said relaxed her, like a good massage. Memories came back to her, in no particular order, but always with an intensity, something essential about returning to her childhood. Internal time is not linear; it is spatial and expansive, following pathways of all directionalities into cavernous, magical and fearful places in the mind.

'I remember one house we were in, Ess,' she says, 'and the children before had left their pet mice. I remember seeing at least six running up and down the pipes.' These creatures were free, playful, having fun. Mum had imagined her family might just be happy there. There are celebrations in her mind, times when she had been part of a school play, and all the children had run out doing the Conga on the playground in triumph once it had finished. She remembers lying in the bath, an iron holdall, the window open, singing opera, always dramatic, always theatrical, while looking on to the undulating hills of the Malverns. And as I listen I can't help thinking that all this drama in her early years will lead to a dramatic death, that she will go out with a bang – which in the end she doesn't.

All these memories are so ingrained in who she is and who she became, yet, despite the detail she is able to retrieve, she can no longer say her name nor her date of birth. We take pieces of paper to every radiography appointment and show it to the radiographers, who are beginning to know Mum and understand her expressive limitations. They don't press her. She shows them the paper, with October written on it. She struggles, 'O, Oc, O, Oc.' It is too much to read the month of her birth. She smiles, knowing that the pressure to perform is unnecessary. Her performance is over, and she must give way to trust. She senses she is in good hands.

There are times during the week of radiography appointments where the small kindnesses of others seem so striking: how, with the utmost decency and care, we are able to notice one another and fill in the gaps intuitively when we can see others struggle. Here in the vastness of the hospital wards, many patients aware of their own suffering seemed more attuned to the suffering of others. One day an elderly gentleman and his wife, so frail and thin, faces deathly pale and eyes hollowed, see that Mum and I are confused by the waiting arrangements for her blood tests. The woman is hunched over herself as if she is forming her own bodily cocoon, into decline rather than beauty, yet she rises to smile and to empathise. 'It's hard to find your way around,' she says. He stands and shows me the way to a ticketing machine, pointing out each sign and to the door that we'll need to enter. Has he noticed Mum's glazed-over, disconnected demeanour: it is possible? These moments are ones in which a deep gratitude comes over me, as well as a horrible fear that others can see that Mum is slowly withdrawing from this world.

For once the blood test is a success: the nurse has found Mum's veins with ease and deep thick red blood streams from them. There is a continuous monitoring – with the chemotherapy – of Mum's blood cell counts. Low blood cell counts can cause serious complications, such as infection, anaemia or bleeding, for people receiving cancer treatment. This constant monitoring is vital, yet so tiring: red, white blood cells, platelets, the need to see that the bone marrow is operating as normally as possible. But for older people like Mum and Dad it means a longer appointment time and more waiting; these are the heroics of medicine, what may for some be one of the big disadvantages to a more stoic way of ending one's days. Yet Mum was warned about quality of life and the balance of pushing on with treatment versus the quiet chirping of birds outside her windows in the cottage. And somehow, strangely, while we are in the hospital together, talking, drinking our hot chocolate, visiting the clothes shop in the huge reception area, bumping into nurses that Mum recognises, there is quality in this. It is the quality of belonging to something bigger, a wandering, transient community of hospital workers and patients. She likes it. On the way home from each radiotherapy treatment she is unstoppable in her chatter, as if she has had a wonderful day trip. How this gives us false hope.

One day we meet with the neurology nurse in the corridor. 'You have been so good to me,' Mum smiles. 'You must make everyone so happy.' The nurse touches Mum gently on the shoulder. A return gift, perhaps, for Mum's unshakeable trust in her. Therapists might think long and hard about accepting a gift from a client; each gift imbued, we imagine, with meaning. But what do we do when the gift is a simple statement?

There is nothing more moving and powerful than a dying client telling you that you are beautiful, when there is nothing skin-deep about it. Of course such a statement might be a learned response to authority figures, the kind of habitual idealising flattery a child perfects as a way into gaining approval from a narcissistic parent. And, yes, this might be worth exploring so that people can free themselves of these internalised relational chains.

But at other times an offering like this needs to be recognised as a gift, a gift of gratitude for the work, for the growth of the human spirit in the face of death. A gift that can in fact be returned, with simplicity, with our acknowledgement, too, that our client is able to love and to give at a time when so much is being taken away. Can we not say, 'I see your beauty, too.'? Is there no better parting gift, in the end, than appreciation, of the type this nurse and Mum had shared?

In hospice care, psychotherapists are lucky to work with others from different disciplines as a way of holding in mind terminally ill people, from the point of view of Cicely Saunders' notion of 'total pain'. Inclusive in her quadrant of needs is someone's spiritual pain. So when we attend rituals to mark the dying of people, for whom we have cared, the spiritual realm poignantly comes into view. We think about the gifts that people will have left us, and those we may have been able to give them before they die.

Some would say that love is a categorical emotion but the more I work with spiritual practitioners, who offer up thoughts from all manner of religious and poetic texts, an example being Rumi's, whose father was a theologian and mystic, the more love seems to be something available to us at all times; as awareness can be. Rumi was known to have said, 'Goodbyes are only for those who love with their eyes, because for those who love with heart and soul there is no such thing as separation.' It stands to reason that when we grieve we become more aware of all the love carried – which quietly existed in our hearts – for those who have died. Since this love is still available to us, after a death, we can make use of it for others who may benefit from our attention, enabling them to experience a sense of 'cosmic specialness' (Becker, 1973) before they die; perhaps something we all seek from the moment we enter the world, a sort of low-level continual trace of our baby self's primary narcissism, which we are too ashamed to acknowledge.

The philosopher Slavoj Zizek (2019) said something like 'Happiness is a by-product, not a goal. If we focus on it we are lost.' This kind of individuated happiness has its place in a neoliberal-based narcissism, which focuses so much on the satisfaction of immediate desire, and construction of image, that it forgets happiness of the type embedded in love, beyond external gaze, which emerges from effortful practice, the mutuality of care and cause, from which we all might benefit. In affirming someone else's 'cosmic specialness' through care, let's say, perhaps we also discover something of our own. Though Rumi's notion of no separation is a little like a phantasised all-engulfing wombspace, without borders, the idea of an undying appreciative love, open to us, could be a radically aware position to take in cut-throat times.

I begin to reflect on how Mum and I are finding or creating our own sense of life's quality in our journeys together up and down in the car, laughing and listening. She tells me off for drinking too much coffee, still my Mum, and I push her slowly in the wheelchair, glad that I have worked in frontline care before. She prompts me to buy a snack and I help her to undo her trousers when she needs me to, this mothering function handed over, and accepted, like a baton in a relay race. And so this in-between place of role reversing finds its own steady rhythm and, though the residual sadness is a constant present which exists just below the surface, we are all right.

At home, Mum relaxes into a greater level of dependency, and I wonder if this is because with me she feels she still has to be mother. With Dad, her identity shifts and she inhabits a more childlike space, more sleepy, less able, more trepidatious about moving at all. In part this mirrors something of the relationship that has always existed between them. Like his mother, my father has always had a caring bent: his reliable presence seemingly allowed Mum to become the powerful teacher she was, supporting her career while perhaps neglecting his own. Now he communicates his patience and reliability silently, as he always has done: in some strange ways nothing between them has really changed.

Care is a funny thing: there is an intimacy in care, in the pragmatic acts of buying someone's favourite foods, in keeping their home warm, in making sure their feet are up. And yet what Dad will come to regret are those moments when he did not put his care into words; that the explicit expression of gratitude was not daily, hourly even. But that is not him: evidence of care always in the action. The comfortable complacent patterns of long marriages sometimes fill us with regret – even though we believe we have known someone when they are gone, we begin to imagine that we had never known them at all – in, at least, all the layers and depths that existed and which perhaps remained unexcavated. We always know and never fully know. When someone has died, there are few that feel they didn't need to know more.

Mum shares a lot with both of us, but I often wonder what she omits to say.

Psychotherapists who work with the dying often become the keepers of memory and secrets; we hold in mind near-complete story books or simply poignant vignettes; we might begin to see patterns and associations between fragments of their lives. Clients sometimes pass on physical manuscripts, or ask us to look through portfolios of paintings, to hear the playlists of songs they have kept, or others scrawl through the collections of photos taken over years on their phones. We bear witness to lives, to lives fading.

Mum often returns to one story that has a deep resonance with her. She had been living in a Nissan hut on the Staverton airbase, a temporary accommodation that had come with her father's new post, after a brief stint of homelessness following his dismissal at a former job. She goes out, a young girl, a cold, white day and begins to build a little house – with rooms inside, a kind of igloo – in the snow. She comes back to this time again and again, to this fantasy of homes and houses, a stark contrast to the partitioned hut she shared with all members of her family, a hut in which drunkards came in at night with her father to gamble. Searching for meaning, I see now home has always been my mother's major preoccupation: rooms, comfort, textiles, design, safety, security, with my father. Abundance.

When she is dead, my father will find one of Mum's poems, *House of Snow*, and we will cry because we knew both the woman and the little girl:

> *Tonight I considered again*
>
> *How to build my house of snow;*
>
> *Push gently at its soft white folds*
>
> *To clear my floors.*
>
> *There could be no walls;*
>
> *No roof could protect me –*
> *And all so very fleeting.*
>
> *Yet within its crushed foundations*
>
> *I could live and be*
>
> *Immeasurably happy.*
>
> *Beyond, there was my wooden world*
>
> *With its match-boxed rooms,*
>
> *So awfully real, so ugly*
>
> *As now, the within was intolerable*
>
> *The without, so preferable.*

It is a privileged role to take up in the lives of terminally ill people: sometimes psychotherapists are the only people to hear these stories, or the only ones who hear the fear, the joys. I wondered about the almost manic push Mum had to tell her stories, and M'Uzan's (2013) thoughts on the 'work of the

dying' which was made possible by the 'surge of libido that…
frequently occurs when death is near' (p. xiii).

Sometimes my mother's vehemence, often perhaps steroid-fuelled, concerns me, the forcefulness of what she says. She tells me how much my husband means to her, how she sees him as a real son. The gratitude is understandable, such is his unwavering support. Then she asks me if he will take an extra name, the name she would have called her own son, had she had one: Daniel. This leaves us in a predicament, a panic. How does one say 'no' to a person who is dying? My husband has his own names already; he does not wish to be claimed by any more parents. We tell her, and despite my mother's intensity she calmly accepts his reasoning; nothing dims, her love for him intact, no sense of personal rejection. Like many dying people, it seemed this was her way of communicating her gratitude, those deepest and often unspoken feelings.

As privileged a position it might be to be a psychotherapist who works with the dying, being privy to people's innermost thoughts can come with a sense of guilt that sometimes the work will not have endured long enough for someone to make those tentative steps towards sharing what's in their minds with those they might have needed to; and so the final intimacies lie with us and not others. This split, in some ways, takes place in our family, though on a minor scale. Dad has perhaps known about much of Mum's life, shared when they were first in love, and courting. Now she tells me, remembering herself as a heartbreaker and a beauty, and how she laughs at this thought. She does not retell these tales to Dad as she becomes more fragile.

In the mornings Mum wakes. 'I have had the most vivid dreams,' she often says. In broken sentences she recounts her wakeful sleep which nonetheless contains lively images of her life flashing before her. There is a clarity to all of this, despite her struggle to retain language. She remembers travelling through France at nineteen: a sequence of train journeys, new friends, a wonderful summer. She had met a Swedish boy named Klaus, who had later been killed in a car accident – like her brother's death, this brutal, abrupt and shocking death had haunted her throughout her life. After a stint running away from the pain of yet another loss, she had worked in Blackpool as a chambermaid. There she met a French student, quite possibly an indirectly serendipitous link to my father, now a student of French at university, and both young women travelled through Dinard, Paris, and on to Lyon. They stayed in the attic of her French friend's aunty, a big roomy space where they giggled and chatted. Chatter and laughter, so much a part of her.

Somewhere in the midst of travel and adventure, she had left her friend to see a French man of her own age, whom she had befriended back in England and whom she had trusted. A gentle, kind man, 'a beautiful soul', quite the contrast to her own father. The relationship was loving but not sexual. 'He opened my eyes to a different side of men, he wanted nothing from me, Esther,' she said. This man would later return to Wales for my mother, to take her hand, but by then it was too late and she had embarked on what would be the relationship with my father that framed her life. From Bordeaux, she made her way back through Paris, crossing the Channel alone and returning to her home town of Cheltenham. College at Swansea would start over again, but not before she entered into a temporary relationship with the owner of a jazz bar. With him, the gentle experience with the French man swung into something more familiar, the jazz bar owner was a hard, exploitative man, and Mum had disappointed herself, ashamed that this older man had taken and used her. She returned to Swansea – despite her earlier adventurous confidence – quietened and alone. A good friend had helped her to rediscover herself and, after a few months, her inner and outer beauty had been confirmed to her by a queue of four or five boyfriends seeking her approval. 'I must,' she says, laughing, 'have been not bad.' All of these memories are flooding back to her in dreamscapes, as if she is there again reliving them. It is as if she is journeying backwards and forwards through her life. This is not uncommon, the striking urgency with which some dying people process a lifetime of memory and attribute meaning to the way their experiences have linked up or come apart.

Her friend at university, Suzanne, was a keen illustrator and had been playing with charcoals one day; she had drawn a man, dark, deep black eyes and hair, a small goatee beard; a sort of French existentialist look. My mother had loved the image. These are the curious synchronicities and associations that a therapist and client in palliative care may start to notice in a life's accounts, but this was my mum and listening to her took on an intensely magical feeling, as I begin to understand the influences on the way my own life had been shaped.

One night in a smoky Welsh pub, Mum had seen my father – a living representation of the image her friend had drawn. With typical forcefulness, she had uttered to Suzanne, 'I am going to marry that man.' Dad followed her out as she left the pub, old raincoat on, black rimmed glasses. There he had made up his own fantasy tale, telling my mother that he had been fighting the colonising forces of the French in Algeria. In reality he had been in hospital in Cimla, Neath, for one year, battling a serious life-threatening bout of tuberculosis, one lung removed, and returning from a desperate experience of dependency, weakness and paralysis.

My parents' marriage, it seemed, was founded from the

very earliest beginnings on the notion of care. Mum devoted herself to feeding my father up, and he in turn took seriously the needs of this emotional waif of a woman who both sought the adoration of men yet pushed them away simultaneously; an ambivalence that had marred her experience as a daughter.

In the summer of their marriage, Mum had been asked to be the university beauty queen, but had refused to do it. Even now, she laughs, in a sort of Foucauldian manner, as if, despite her beauty then, this was not the order of things for her; an out-of-category jarring moment in her life. Or perhaps now as she is, even plumper with steroids, old and increasingly incapacitated, that time is so far removed from the reality of now. 'It wasn't my scene at all, darling,' she giggles.

She repeats the minutiae of a first year of married life in a caravan, elemental, above the surf of the Gower Peninsula, arguments about the cold and the heating, erratic neighbours who planted dead mice at their door. I am knowing her again and again, a series of mnemic ghosts, or what Yalom (2008) might consider 'ripples', that will become my present and past and future. Bracha Ettinger (2006), writing on the matrixial, about the way that we relate always to each other's internal psychic resonance fields, made up of traces of histories of people in our network, comes to mind in these days that we spend together.

Dad is glad of the week's respite; I can see that. The burden of care is of course heavy for all those who are informally propping up the State, with its dearth of robust social care. In the UK one in eight adults are carers: this makes up 6.5 million people who are taking on the caring responsibility of those in need. 58% are women; 42% men – 1.3 million people providing over fifty hours of care per week, saving the economy £132 billion per year. Often unacknowledged, and shamed into the shadows of their role, often having left work behind, 72% of carers responding to Carer UK's 'State of Caring 2018' reported that they had suffered mental ill health as a result of caring. In the work we do as psychotherapists in palliative care we see how high this burden can be – the social isolation, the awful guilt about resenting vulnerable dependents, the sleepless nights. Dad is tired, partially because his care seems to be so devoted; and yet because he is imperfect, as we all are, I fear that in his grief he will focus more on his failings than on his commitment, on those moments where he turns his head away or uses a prickly tone.

I depart the cottage, after this week of accompanying Mum to radiotherapy, to return home to our family, and Mum and Dad will carry on with the journeys to the hospital for another week. Dad will be glad when all these visits give way to something simpler.

Decline and dependency

As my routine momentarily returns to normal – the school drop-offs, the making of tea, the drives to various activities, work with clients – so Dad and Mum continue the treatment. Things are somehow getting harder – I can hear it in Dad's voice – and Mum will not come to the phone, saying 'hello' only from the background. She is no longer centre stage, as if she is slipping behind the curtain of her own life.

At the beginning of the week, she has an appointment with the consultant. Anxiety around her bulging legs, which had already been treated with antibiotics for fear of infection, means that the consultant and nurse decide to stop Mum's chemo. This is the bumpy ride of cancer that many clients receiving palliative care know about: the hope followed by the dashed hope; the belief in the continuation of life interrupted by a step closer to death. I want to rage and tell Dad to challenge this, that Mum's legs were on the mend, that this is over-cautious, that, that, that… surely she must finish, she must buy time…

I seem to hold for the family the voice of medical heroics despite all I know, all the learning about the value of calmly accepting and relinquishing the control over life: what tension is this to sit with… Mum is unrattled, and Dad explains that the infected legs could have turned septic. It's precautionary. I have the foreboding sense that Mum will soon succumb to this glioblastoma and we will say goodbye: her body and mind disintegrating slowly before us. For us it seems our role will increasingly be about being alongside Mum as she moves into greater states of dependency, as peacefully as we can.

Peace and psycho-spirituality

In palliative care, we sometimes talk about the work being psycho-spiritual in that it straddles personal histories while also attempting often to unpack those blocking habitual grooves of behaviour in patients and families. This is done in tandem with searching for meanings in this life and sometimes beyond. The once Harvard psychologist and Buddhist practitioner, Ram Dass (2001), who died just before Christmas 2019, spent his life bringing under one roof the psychological and spiritual, leading to the creation, among other things, of the Living/Dying project, a space for exploration in the face of a terminal illness. The ebb and flow of the psycho-spiritual was also found in the words of one of his students, psychiatrist and pioneer in near-death studies, Elizabeth Kubler-Ross (1969), whose sometimes misunderstood stage-model of death and dying has been hugely influential in palliative care.

But what am I getting at here? I suppose it is this: that we are born into the world and we are, over time, initiated into discursive processes that we absorb and which condition us into making certain choices and behaving in certain ways. Often such discourses are inscribed into our very being and often we mistake such narratives as our own, as if our identity hinges on a rule book that, ultimately, was never ours in the first place. This is not to suggest that we abandon our responsibility to one another; rather the effort is in treading carefully as we discover our personal freedoms in this context of interconnected responsibility.

We cannot plaster over our understandings of who we are with spiritual practice if our emotional depths are left unexplored; our gods will often excuse us and allow us to repeat any damage; but in the world of death and dying neither can we inhabit the psychological alone without beginning to travel into the mystery of each day, the soul of people's experience, and what Carl Jung (1963) might describe as 'synchronistic phenomena, premonition and dreams that come true'. What Ram Dass (2001) tells us in his grounded and grounding book, *Still Here*, on ageing and dying is that in order to go on being, with the highest level of integrity, we need to switch between two sets of language (or alternative discourses) where our emotional conditioning is put under the microscope regularly and where our experience of the phenomenology of existence – as a small particle in this immense space – is also tapped into at an unconscious, embodied level. The former perhaps brings us to a place of compassion for ourselves and others; the latter allows us to let go of ourselves, as we note the fragility of our egotistical selves – and both no doubt help us to love, to live and to die. In some ways, spending time with my mother over that week of radiotherapy seemed to be in alignment with this notion of psychological excavation, its repetition, and the relinquishing of masks in order to peacefully depart.

I hear about my friend's dad with a glioblastoma still going to the pub, and I am happy for her while sad that my mother can barely walk out into the garden now. I hear that his personality is changing. It is not uncommon for new character traits to emerge, the result of major changes to the structure of the brain. We hear of people who were once mild-mannered becoming cantankerous, former men and women of the church cursing family and friends. Tumours might play havoc with a patient's frontotemporal lobes, leading to disinhibition and bringing forth all the repressed wild feelings once stored away. I chat with my friend, and wonder how long each of us has with our parents. It is strange how community can form in pain; how both of us inhabit a dying space yet the excited energy of our children invariably interrupt our pensive conversations.

Mum's treatment now over, there is a wait of a month until she sees the oncologist to determine how the tumour has responded to chemo. We all wish it were sooner, but the treatment is said to go on – hopefully – shrinking the tumour in that time, so a scan now would be premature.

In the weeks leading up to the appointment, Mum's speech becomes more and more evasive, her language more akin to that of a kindergarten child than a woman whose linguistic cadences could be musical, who taught sometimes illiterate children to enjoy the works of Steinbeck, Harper Lee, the Brontes. She tires. She speaks to me for only minutes on the telephone now, and I am beginning to miss her greatly although she is still alive. As cancer took hold of Freud (1925), he noted his increasing exhaustion and began to welcome it in:

I am as weary as it is natural to be after a hard-working life, and I think I have fairly earned my rest. The organic elements that have held together for so long are tending to fall apart. Who would wish them to remain forcibly connected any longer? Sigmund Freud *(letter to Pfister)*, 1925

Mum has small wins now, and these form the moments of meaning in each day. 'I wash my face every night; arms out and hands out. It's red,' she says. What the redness signifies I do not know, but these accounts of hers signify perhaps that the little moments of independence bring some colour to the day. Or perhaps red is simply code for 'great'. In those who are dying, it is often important to notice and to honour those capacities that are retained, to manage our own anxiety in the face of their decline so that we do not take over, becoming overbearing, a helicopter carer, infantilising and risk-averse. And yet the temptation is to fill in all the gaps, as a way to control our own fears and anxiety; perhaps to protect us from the pain of watching someone we love become slower, less able, less their former selves.

Therapists working in palliative care are exposed to their fair share of human pain each day and, in line with perhaps our bent for rescuing and the invaluable ongoing supervision we need, most therapists will not become inured, will not become hardened, to another's distress, no matter how unbearable that may be. What we might experience is our own process of self-fragilisation (Ettinger, 2009) where we become porous, stirred up – what Bion (1962) might have described as 'reverie' or what Ram Dass (2001) might term 'open-heartedness' – in the face of another's raw undigested feeling, yet we do not crumble under the weight of it. Rather we try – in our work, at least

– to sit with those heavy feelings in the room, acknowledge their affect inside and then offer reflections, both client and therapist together at times making a challenge to the other; both, you might hope, learning. Neither person in the room is the authority, just two human beings sharing perspectives on a particular strand of narrative or experience.

Sometimes, though, the exercise of therapy takes place at a more primitive level: therapy becomes a holding space, a bearing witness, a simple mirroring to the pain. The reflective element, the move to interpretation is an unnecessary intrusion, its presence perhaps felt as a persecutory object. So some days are days of holding. Of being alongside histories of parental alcoholism or suicide, of shifting fearful eyes, of long slogs in police vans or psychiatric units, racist, physical or sexual trauma and abuse, stillborns and self-harm – and all this underpinning someone's terminal illness; all this buried and yet strangely close to the surface. And you wonder to yourself if the role of the therapist is sometimes no more than the offering of a trusted space, a reliable space, in which some safety can be found in the outside world. An outside world from which threat once came, but which now has moved inwards to inhabit this person's body with disease; the body in the last years or months or weeks cruelly becoming that final threat, so sadly symbolic of a history of attack and precariousness. So often our people, brutalised by life's events and the bullying hands that once touched them, demonstrate the kind of courage most of us can only dream of, their spirits indomitable, their kindnesses, their capacity to show love towards others in the face of death a sign of dignity where others might have become animal. Sometimes, as a therapist, you really can go home and weep at the sheer amazingness of the human beings you encounter.

All this while, Mum has said she will live until the end of March. She wants to last to see our daughter make her first appearance on stage, in the amateur performance of *Oliver*. Dad is reticent. Mum has fallen twice now and he senses that she is unbalanced. He is frightened of more of these falls where he cannot help her to get back up. She is a weight, a dead weight in fact, and only a call-out to the paramedics can get her back on her feet. He cannot bear the indignity of her collapsing, and shuffling along the cold tiled floor on her behind – as she has done – to try to get to the comfort of a carpeted room. Dad is traumatised by the drama of it all, and his own frightening helplessness, which undoubtedly mirrors my Mum's, in the face of hers.

But she is determined and, on Saturday 30 March, they both come. The musical is brilliant, Eloise at home on the stage among friends. Mum is smiling, constantly, muddled but very alive.

We have the photograph of her now, wheelchair-bound, clutching the brochure, trying so hard to read it, to spot our daughter's face. She is full of joy, throughout the performance, but leaves before the crowds depart. The day after this I will travel home, a huge bunch of flowers – gerberas, a fuchsia pink one that she tries to eat – for Mother's Day, a day that has always been a little neglected in our family, a protest against the commercialisation of love.

And when I leave her, having sat a few hours on her bed, next to her, I drive home in tears. All these lasts are beginning to sink in; a recognition that soon they will be nothing but vivid images that I will repeat, no doubt, in order to let go.

A GOOD DEATH?

'*A good death doth honour to a whole life.*'
Petrarch (1304)

'*Doesn't the final meaning of life, too,
reveal itself, if at all, only at its end,
on the verge of death?*'
Viktor Frankl (1959)

I t was at the beginning of the Easter holidays that things
took a turn for the worse. Having finished the three-week
treatment of palliative radiotherapy and the combined, yet
unfinished, tablets of chemotherapy, Mum waited at home until
she had a meeting with the oncologist. At this stage, we were
all still living in some kind of tentative hope that the tumour
may have shrunk with those twenty-one days of focused blasts
to the site. Dad and Mum had been pootling through life,
making short visits to the local shops, eating three meals a day,

one or two steps in the breezy winds of Selsey Common, an ancient place with breath-taking views over the River Severn and Malvern Hills into Wales.

Even on the afternoon before what was to be, in reality, the beginning of the end, Dad and Mum had made it on to the Common. We might imagine them strolling past the hawthorn, blackthorn and beech, noticing the wild orchid that spring up in the sites of former quarries, or commenting on the grasslands or a Saxon tale of enclosed land. But this was not the case, Mum had left the car and taken two steps, allowed the freshness of the air to cool that youthful skin of hers and then suggested she return to the car. On that day she was low of energy and stamina.

As was their daily routine, they had returned home, eating a small lunch and then taking a nap in the afternoon. To all intents and purposes, though both knew that brain cancer had forced such momentous change to their lives, the gentle ticking along of their retired days continued without drama. Until that evening.

My father had woken at 2am in the morning, hearing the faint calling out of my mother. 'Phil' we might imagine her calling, or 'Bunge', a nickname that had been in existence since I was a child. Or it is possible that some unknown sound was used, given the slips and slides of Mum's speech. Whichever it was, Dad had rushed downstairs. There was Mum, her head and chest pushed into the safety bars that were now attached to her hospital bed, for fear of her falling. The lower half of her body was precariously hanging from the bed, her legs somehow cut and bleeding. Dad thought that Mum had been trying to get hold of her walking stick to make one of her regular late night visits to the toilet, but somehow – and at this point it was unclear how – she had lost her strength or forgotten the sequence of the movements she needed to make. Now his wife was hanging over the side of the bed, like a car hanging over a cliff face, the balance death-defying, precarious. Trying with all his might to move my mother back into a position of safety, on the mattress top, my father was now beginning to lose his own strength and soon Mum slipped out of his arms, falling entirely to the floor. This was now the third fall she had had with what now, in retrospect, seemed to be the sheer impact of the brain tumour.

At this point, Dad had settled Mum on the floor surrounded by cushions, realising he would only be able to return her to bed with the help of some burly paramedics and an inflatable contraption that could raise her from the floor. He made the call. It was a night of crisis, the third of the falls signalling greater proximity to ultimate collapse. At this stage, there were no signs of seizure; it looked simply as if Mum – doing her nightly walks to the toilet that her own mother before her had used when living in my parent's home – had become either disoriented or unstable. The fragility, as far as I could gather, was located more in my father, whose sleep – never good – was now practically non-existent, whose physical strength was diminishing in relation to the difficulty of supporting my mother.

Dad had protected me, resisting making a call in the middle of the night. My mother now back in bed, and at least safe, so my father imagined, would come round in the morning and engage with the world afresh, wanting her routine breakfast of honey on bread with a hot chocolate at 11am. He imagined that the days would unfold, carer and cared-for, dancing around each other, as they had done before this fall. My father had convinced himself, as he later told me, that he could have gone on for an age, responding to my mother's simple needs. Psychotherapist Juliet Rosenfeld (*Guardian,* February 2020), experienced in working with struggling bereaved people, looks back on her husband's death and is 'still perplexed by the strength of his denial' and by her own 'complicity'. Such is our denial, perhaps, when we want someone to go on forever.

But my mother did not rouse herself that next morning, and so, by 10am at my desk awaiting a family who were struggling with news of the father's growing tumour behind his eyes, and feeling they had been complacent in their belief he would 'beat cancer', I got a call from my father. 'Mum doesn't seem to be coming round, you better come home soon.' It is an awful feeling to be pulled in different directions: clients – much younger than my own parents, small children – who are seeking the space to communicate honestly without entirely losing hope and breaking each other's spirit; ageing parents who needed both a daughter and a partial professional to do some kind of overall assessment; children of my own, who would soon lose a grandparent. These moments of crisis make it hard to slow down, and maintain the space in one's mind to be able to think, but at the same time this was needed.

Stepping more into the role of a psychotherapist than a daughter, I listened to my father's voice; was my mother dying imminently? What had the palliative care professionals on his end expressed? In essence, there was some hope: the palliative care coordinator, an efficient procedural professional, had explained that it was possible that my mother had had an acute episode in response to the intense series of radiotherapy she had received; that her brain had perhaps expanded and caused a series of seizures, unseen, that she might recover from. This was, in this most grim situation, the one sign of hope. Alternatively, the change in my mother – now unspeaking and asleep – was the beginning of the end of life; the pathway of final care might well be triggered, the gentle monitoring and offering of responsive comfort care. We did not know.

Having seen a client's family, whose complex inter-subjective dynamics were hard to sit with, yet whose awkwardness around their own emotional worlds were understandable, I would go home to my mother and my father, whose anxiety was palpable yet whose words conveyed a sort of fantastical belief in the power of healing not dissimilar to the man I had seen that morning. Dad's father had been a Presbyterian minister who laid hands on the ill with the hope of cure and salvation. Though Dad was an atheist, these experiences were strangely brought back to life in the way that Dad gently pressed the palm of his hand on Mum's head, as if he could reawaken her.

Kubler-Ross (1969) in her stage-driven model of coming to terms with a terminal diagnosis understood denial to be a natural, albeit sometimes high-stake, response to the news of a patient who is told they will die of their condition. On many levels, she believed that to be in denial at first is not necessarily overly defensive, but rather allows people to maintain a level of hope as they navigate the uncertainty of their predicament. Though my own mother had, momentarily, exhibited an optimism that the tumour had perhaps abandoned her – particularly during the days in hospital waiting for the biopsy – overall her acceptance of dying had been notable. As a result, I wondered if her speed of acceptance was also something to do with a fatalism which stemmed from the early loss of her own brother, and a silent, almost impermeable, stoicism that she had experienced in her own mother. Hope, and its relationship with denial, was located in my father: he envisaged his wife going on for much longer, longer even than the projected months the consultants had given. It stood to reason, given Dad's year-long recovery from tuberculosis, that he needed to guard himself against thoughts of death and dying. Both my parents were, in different ways, affected in their lives by loss and the possibility of loss, a dread of death, that might unconsciously have become my own. Such are the ways that histories among family members are shared, repeated, re-scripted.

> The force of his denial means that she begins to embody all the death anxiety in the room, in her shakiness and near-constant tears, all the fears and imagined sadness of his ultimate parting. The silence around his distress makes her anxiety louder: she is angry that he has shut down to reality and he in turn is angry that she is puncturing his tightly held together appearance of equilibrium with her overwhelm. How do we achieve greater balance, a less fraught outcome for the family?

And so when I returned home after the session that I had managed to facilitate that morning, for the first time, my father's optimism was hanging in the balance. Tears were welling up in his eyes, 'Ess, I think she is on her way out.'

As I entered the study, the small world that had become Mum's, she was lying asleep and still, eyes closed, serene looking. I stroked her hair, some silver strands coming loose, but there was no movement. It seemed the case that Mum might soon die.

That night was one of the worst nights of my life.

The atmosphere at home, just Dad and I, was quiet. Neither of us knew what might happen in the following hours or days. We drank tea and ate noodles, crisps and nuts on autopilot, as if we knew that we would have to replenish ourselves but that we were barely taking nourishment in.

We decided that one of us should sleep next to Mum each night and so we brought a bed down from upstairs, one which had always been in the room my parents called the playroom – a space full of curious toys that had been collected over the years for our children. Some of them had travelled from our home to my parents' and others had been selected with utmost care by Mum, who had enjoyed finding rag dolls with big wide smiles and handmade booties so unlike the broken doll of her childhood.

The bed itself was a bed within a bed. A single that could be converted into a double, a secondary bed which lived under the more stable one, reminding one of partnerships and the way that resilience can be distributed among a pair. Dad and I brought down the single mattress and the folding legs that brought the second bed to a decent waist-like height. We placed it next to Mum who was still in a deep, restful place on the hospital bed that had fast become her limited world.

I had been pained to see this happen to clients over the course of their illnesses, when the fatigue and progression of a condition had started to take its final hold. Family members had often redesigned rooms downstairs. Studies or lounges becoming bedrooms, with equipment such as hoists, beds with pressure-relieving mattresses, commodes, changed spaces accommodating changed people. Those more able imagine extending their homes to accommodate a dying space, talking about stair lifts and easy access showers months and months before it might be necessary.

Being the partner of someone who is dying with a life-limiting condition means that your entire life begins to centre around them, often a partner's life becoming confined and narrow too: the outside world ends up being about picking up prescriptions, doing small food shops, meeting with nurses and medical professionals. I have known partners to move in – rather as my father had done – to these newly reconfigured spaces in homes, reading there, watching television, working on laptops by the side of the unwell person. And this can last for days, weeks, months. Such is our attachment to people we love and care about, the anxiety of separation determining our every action. Esther Perel (2007) talks about the continual human tension between wanting stability and yearning for excitement and change. For partners of terminally ill people, this tension often continues but desire of novelty, discontinuity, pleasure is soured by a profound sense of guilt; a residual question of how can I possibly feel sorry for myself for not going out, travelling, dancing when my partner will soon no longer breathe? Stability, in these circumstances, will always come before desire.

> *Intimacy between them is hard. He comes back from a short trip, and she is angered by his absence, despite the timetable of care he has set up. Yet the space between them is not just physical and, apart, some reflection has taken place. She wishes to talk to him again, the kind of closeness she needs. He doesn't talk, but asks that they can experience their naked bodies together again. She understands his communication of tenderness, but for her there will be no pleasure: her body aches, she is cold, her movements wooden. Their sense of intimacy and intimacies hinge on such very different understandings now.*

As I held my mother's arm, breathing deeply into the night, I remember thinking about how she had endured this ordeal. She had shown no anxiety throughout, and I wondered if some part of her had known that her time was coming to an end. Or whether she was a woman in two parts: wife, mother, grandmother who would have continued for many more years to be there in our joys and our disappointments; and the woman who had lived with great physical pain long before the knowledge of the tumour's existence. Both joined, now; Mum seemed ready to go.

I touched the skin on her arm, a plump arm with freckles, and I found myself hauling myself up to look at her sleeping face, placing my cheek next to hers.

Like those first nights with a newborn baby – the waking states, the watching of a chest moving up and down, the snuffling noises – for those who sit by the side of the dying, a tension rises up. There is a need for sleep, the bearing witness to decline is heavy and exhausting, but there is also a residual concern that each micro-movement conveys meaning: pain, thirst, death.

Eventually, I must have drifted into sleep. But in the early hours, I heard a strange and unfamiliar rattling sound. Opening my eyes, in the hazy pimpled blackness, I could see my mother jerking, her right-hand side flailing about in the bed, her arm slapping the wall next to her. Still her face, perfectly still. I called out to her, 'Mum,' but there was nothing.

Her leg, also on the right side, was making shaking, fidgeting movements. This was not twitching, but something more forceful, the whole right hand side of her body banging. I leaned over and tried to hold on to her, I gently reassured her that I was next to her, that it would be all right, but I didn't know. I was no medic. I wanted to be able to soothe her, as I had soothed my daughter and son in the early hours of their newborn cries, but Mum was not hungry or cold or wide-awake, she was desperately unwell and this was some kind of seizure, of which I had no understanding.

I called for Dad. He arrived bleary eyed, long johns on, remembering the catastrophic seizure she had had on Boxing Day. I asked him if the woman from the palliative care team had left any medications to get this under control. Torn between wanting to call in professionals and knowing that Mum would not want to be moved to a hospital environment, we carefully located buccal midazolam, which was to be given to Mum in the buccal cavity of her mouth between her cheek and the gum. I administered the drug, and waited. Slowly the seizures eased, her arm stopped banging as forcefully against the wall, me bending over her and holding it as still as I could all the while.

The medication was such a relief to have, and I realised then how important the placing of what Community Nurse Specialists call anticipatories, or 'just in case' medication, were. It was for a panicked emergency such as this one, a way of ensuring that family members could respond, to have something there in the immediacy. It staved off the full unbearable helplessness of watching someone you love in pain, struggling to right themselves. Often the medication is for pain, breathlessness, sickness and vomiting or agitation. That night, we also had a liquid form of anti-seizure medication, which we could offer Mum. NICE Guidelines on End of Life Care (2017), for adults in the last days of life, explain the rationale for having anticipatory medication in the home, as follows:

> As a person approaches the last few days of their life, changes in their condition may lead to changes in existing symptoms, the emergence of new symptoms or changes in the person's ability to take medicines to manage their symptoms (such as swallowing oral medicines). Prescribing medicines in anticipation can avoid a lapse in symptom control, which could otherwise cause distress for the person who is dying and those close to them.

To see the force of Mum's banging arm, jerking leg, slow to a twitch was a relief. We took deep breaths. Dad made us an early morning – it was now 2am – cup of tea. We might have wanted to sleep now.

This was not to be the case. Shortly after Dad had made his way back upstairs and I had turned the light off, returning to bed, touching Mum's arm again, not wanting to let her go, the seizures recommenced, with the same power and force. A strange smell seemed to accompany the fitting and I wondered what this was; I imagined that death leaked out of people, and gave those around an olfactory sign that the last minutes were on the horizon. It was as if the breath that Mum was releasing from her mouth was a toxic cloud of illness, and my mind did somersaults about what was taking place. Again I spoke to her and whispered to Mum that we would calm things down shortly. She didn't seem conscious, no signs of pain on her expressionless face. This seemed to be the most important thing; so long as Mum was unaware, making no sounds of distress, then it seemed that Dad and I would be able to find enough peace in ourselves to be able to comfort her, to keep her with us at home.

We had read on the buccal bottle that we could administer the liquid again. I placed the syringe, with its orangey liquid, into Mum's mouth. After five to ten minutes the seizures started to slow. Only ten minutes passed before her body began rattling violently again.

We called 111. A series of questions followed, determining whether Mum was unconscious or not, what medication had she had, how often were the seizures. I was on the phone and counting her fits simultaneously, counting the fits of the woman who had once nursed me in her arms.

Dad made more tea, fearful perhaps of what was to come; needing to just *do*.

The paramedics arrived. A huge, wide, red-faced man,

relatively young, thick West Country accent, and to the point; a younger woman, efficient, slender, hair pulled back; and another taller woman, more perceptive, slow, noticing, glasses on, capable but kind.

Bags placed on the sofa, equipment pulled out, oxygen masks – attached to a tank – placed gently on Mum's face, SATS taken, oxygen levels low. There is discussion around her bed. For the male paramedic, this is an emergency and Mum's best place is in hospital. 'We need to take her in, really,' he says. I explain that in her notes, on her advance care plan she is categorical that she does not want to go into hospital for treatment, for resuscitation, for anything that will prolong her life if she is reaching the end.

People who have toiled against disease begin to wish that the struggle is over. In multi-disciplinary meetings across the UK, nurses and doctors, social workers, counsellors will discuss the 'wishes' of their patients; this will be recorded on databases, in files, to capture the views of those who are dying. It is a curious thought that someone chooses not to have interventions that might save his or her life, or to prolong life even if it is just for a few days. But terminal illness is often an experience of endurance, far removed from the daily life, pleasures and meanings that one may have had.

Dying wishes

Campaigners for assisted dying cite cases where people want to die prematurely, to avoid a difficult, messy and painful death. In 2019, Dignity in Dying released a hard-hitting short film, alongside their report, 'Inescapable Truth', written by King's College scholars, Parry and Eales (2019), which found that seventeen people died in horrific circumstances each day. Having presented hospice provision bleakly in the film, a huge furore erupted over Twitter, with a series of open letters penned by Tracey Bleakely of Hospice UK and Sarah Wootten of Dignity in Dying. A worrying splitting emerged between those seemingly idealising dying and those depicting horrendous, anxiety-provoking deaths; underpinning these conceptualisations and narratives were different values, agendas and beliefs: broadly, a belief in the desire for control versus the possibility of acceptance. Speaking about death and dying, it was clear, evoked powerful feelings in professionals, patients and lay people alike.

Now the burly paramedic seemed ill at ease with talking about Mum's death so openly. Mum was clear that if she reached a state in which she was no longer able to communicate in words, or move physically, she was ready to die. We showed the paramedics the file which the palliative care team had left in situ: in it were her hand-written and signed wishes. We talked it over with the team, the male paramedic still nervous about the suggestion that Mum stay at home to be as comfortable as possible. The large female paramedic understood, nodded her head: she had seen this before. She talked about how we would want to get the seizures under control, that perhaps now our family would be best off in the hands of the district nurse.

The thin young paramedic moved around, shifting things in the bag, which seemed like a displacement activity for her discomfort. She was also new to the job. In the meantime, the male – apparently the lead – called in his superiors and told them Mum's illness trajectory, the prognosis, the current seizures. Dad was in the shadows listening, but in shock, standing at the foot of Mum's bed, watching her breathe. All this time I had been stroking Mum's arm and face, turning to her as if

I wanted her to tell me that this was the right decision for this terrifying moment, that perhaps it was time to accept that perhaps nothing could be done.

It was decided that Mum remain in the familiarity of her home. Far from being the officious, almost blunt, professional we had first encountered, the paramedic finished his call, whispering, 'This is hard, this is really hard, but I am glad that for once we are able to follow someone's wishes.' He was visibly moved, as if he had learned something he might have wanted to close himself off to. I think he could see that the human must always foreground the procedural, the task. Bertrand Russell once said, 'The thing I mean is love, or compassion. If you feel this, you have a motive for existence, a reason for courage, a guide in action.' The young paramedic had shown courage, and in that moment something human was guiding him.

For us, it was, in some ways, as if Mum were already dead. Ordinarily she would have spoken at this point, thanked the paramedics for coming, for responding. She'd have said something sentimental, and we'd have laughed. But she was still unconscious, here in her twitching physical body, present, yet unavailable, beyond reach.

In academic circles, the very idea of death itself is a contested one. Individuals, different cultures and communities respond to the question of death in varying ways, with myriad understandings of what death might be, the whys, whens and how long? The process of defining death perhaps also requires us to define life, and at what point a life may end. With Mum on her bed, lying speechless like this, her life as she had once known it was at an end, and my father and I would have to try to adjust over the coming days or weeks, to this version of Mum.

Of course, biological death is that very final, permanent cessation of vital functions, which ends life in the physical body and the breath that keeps us linked to existence. It seemed that Mum was now at least in some kind of transitional space; or what medics might have referred to as brain-dead, or in the grey zone perhaps, as it is known. People from other cultures might disagree completely: for the Tana Torajans, even the skeletal mummified bodies of ancestors that join them at their table for lunch are not fully dead, but rather on a spiritual journey into the afterlife (Doughty, 2017). Death is just one step towards a greater mystery.

For us in the West, influenced as we are by Descartes, the dualistic mind-body split, it would logically follow that Mum might be judged, now without her functioning brain, to be no longer with us. Descartes described himself as a 'thing that thinks'. His essence, he claimed, consisted 'in this alone, that I am a thinking thing, as a substance whose whole essence or nature consists in thinking' (Descartes, 1968, p. 156). The notion of the individual, who proves his own existence by a process of methodological self-certification, is at the heart of Descartes' philosophy; a logical subject who is enclosed, isolated, and separated from his own sensory possibilities and learning, and outside the material world.

'My mind, which alone, I take now as being myself, is enclosed.' (Descartes, 1968 p. 128)

Existence, for Descartes, related to the sovereignty of mind over body, and indeed other bodies (or objects) in the material world. Historically speaking, men of Descartes' generation also had a desire to dominate and to control the irrational, not dissimilar to these neoliberal times. This construction of mind led to a distinctive kind of subject-object split, in which the subject was master and possessor of the object (or of Nature, if we consider the time Descartes was writing). Watching Mum, it was as if this neat Cartesian division was no longer applicable; and as she slept and breathed it seemed increasingly that she was simply being, a part of Nature, barely separate from it. Through her, the pulse of existence beat, as it does for us all.

We could argue that a Cartesian way of thinking about people who are unconscious is related to our social norms, the discursive practices and narratives we take in and reinforce over time: after all, the brain is arguably considered the most important organ in the human body: it provides a home for the rational mind; relatedly, a controlling, cognisant, autonomous, self-actualising being.

And yet for my father and I – sitting there as we did, awaiting the district nurse now that the paramedics had left, with yet another cup of tea in hand – this woman, my mother, had more value now than ever, as we acknowledged her place, fully embodied in our lives. Mum was not mind, it seemed, but embodiment of so much experience. She was becoming more akin to Merleau Ponty's subject, that through the body, her body, there was a 'means by which consciousness is situated in the world' (Spurling, 1977, p. 21). She continued to be, for us, a being-in-the-world, constituted not from substance but through the relational field of body-and-world. A relational field that, despite her unconscious state, existed around her. So, from this angle, Mum was still very much alive.

Not long after the paramedics left, Mum now stabilised with oxygen and yet more liquid buccal midazolam, we had a visit from a heavy-set district nurse, her auburn wavy hair pulled back in a ponytail. Behind the professionalism of her uniform, it was clear to see that she was naturally warm: under any other circumstances you could imagine her joking and laughing, and pulling friends inwards towards her substantial bosom.

I distracted myself from how upsetting our predicament was by imagining her dressed as a Victorian scullery maid, working in the depths of one of those palatial National Trust homes with cool, white kitchens and larders. Such tricks the mind plays when in a panic. My parents' home was becoming staffed by so many different people, in different uniforms, with different roles; there was both comfort and confusion in this.

During the 1960s and 1970s, in counterpoint to the medicalisation of death, the hospice movement began to develop a new articulation of a good death, frequently conceptualised as the 'revivalist good death' (Seale, 1998; Walter, 1994). Borgstrom (2014), and Cottrell and Duggleby (2016) proposed a number of features that are often associated with the notion of the good death in western cultures. Beyond a preparedness and acceptance of death, minimal pain, and the resolution of difficult issues, one major feature linked to the notion of a good death is the possibility of dying in familiar surroundings with family members close by. This is, most definitely, what my mother had wanted, and so we attempted as well as we could have done to respect her choice to die at home.

Written into the Western conceptualisation of a good death are the tenets of choice and control, resonating with overarching socio-political discourses that foreground 'autonomy, authenticity, individualization, self-determination, quality of life and self-realization as core values' (Jacobsen and Dalgaard, 2013, p. 310). These ideals also underpin a Western construction of what makes up a good life, now perhaps simply applied to the process of dying. The logic follows, then, that in neoliberal individualistic climes, a bad death might be one where a person has no autonomy, is unable to make rational decisions, owing to a lack of capacity and the inability to communicate his or her wishes.

However, the latter are the preoccupations of an individualistic culture to be understood critically, embedded as they are in a Eurocentric set of values, informing our attitudes towards dying. A good death for some societies, on the contrary, is one in which a person dies in service of his country or religion, for example (Rosenblatt, 2008). For those who believe in reincarnation, death may implicitly always-already be good because the ending of the body signifies a rebirth of the spirit, the possibility of another chance in the karmic wheel. We know that practices around dying also differ among cultures: in Western societies, a comfortable bed may arguably be the preferred place of death, with select family members by the side. In Hinduism, those who are dying might make their way to the floor to be closer to Mother Earth, so that the soul can leave the body with greater ease.

Yet it seemed strange to me that in Mum's dying, she did seem to engender those rationalistic and Eurocentric values on one level while her acceptance of death spoke to something altogether more mystical and spiritual. That said, her choices were never made in isolation, and emerged out of discussions with the family and with professionals who effectively became part of our wider system, a series of concentric circles moving out beyond Mum.

Though the mantra of choice and control had always been a problematic one for me to subscribe to, I could see now that for my mother – whose childhood had been depicted by an absence of personal control and possibly felt-voicelessness – choice was something she wished to retain to the end of her life.

However, for my father, in supporting my mother's choice to die at home, he had less control. Though he never complained, the home he had known as a private space – with just him and his wife quietly pottering around one another – soon became a public one. At times up to ten people would visit in a day. For some this would be intolerable, a frantic merry-go-round of faces. My father, though, an introverted man, responded openly to all of his visitors, and it became clear that he was glad of the support. And so a strange paradox was evident: Mum had no control over the fact that she was dying, her tumour multiplying, and yet in setting out her advance care plan the network of care was supporting her choices. Yet her choices were arguably forcing my father into a position of having less choice and control about the structure and routine of his day and his home life. The dynamics of choice.

Notions of choice and control seep into our consciousness, a normativising discourse against which we might judge ourselves. What happens to a person with brain cancer, without family, unable to think of his or her impending death, who struggles with the filling out of forms, inarticulate in the domain of choice? Would he be left feeling like a failure for not having prepared, for not having taken control?

It is perhaps wise at this stage to wonder if this limited conceptualisation of a good death may inadvertently push us into taking control at a time in our lives where we might rather be guided by others, allow ourselves to depend and to trust, to relinquish control. French philosopher Michel Foucault (2010) would have suggested that 'the good death' was a kind of discursive impingement, known as 'governmentality', a process by which people can be controlled, paradoxically and powerfully, through an imagined 'freedom' to do the societal right thing.

I digress. Back to the wonderful district nurse, who, with us, spends the evening awake in our home for several hours as we watch over Mum, who has now had anti-seizure medication injected directly into her stomach. Watching the injection enter her stomach, and seeing no grimace on her face, was unbearable; Mum's body itself generating no sign of human agency, no flinching, no movement as the needle punctured her skin.

An expression of sadness came over the nurse's face, and no doubt our own, and we stopped to talk about whether these were my mother's final hours. The nurse felt that this was something she had seen before, the more laboured breath, the deep unconsciousness and so we became quiet, trying to take in the enormity of what she was saying, what she was expecting.

Once the seizures were under control, the district nurse took her leave, but reminded us of the emergency numbers we could call – the out-of-hours professionals that would be busy working their shifts – that we must not hesitate to be in touch. She left in a sombre mood, and my father and I slipped into a sort of silent calm. I returned to the put-up bed, and dad returned upstairs. We were now in wait.

It can be very hard for families to sit in the uncertainty with someone dying, those times when professionals depart and a sense of aloneness engulfs those in the room. The questions that we might entertain: will there be a lot of blood, some kind of haemorrhage? How will I know when the breath changes? Will he or she be in pain?

For others, relationships with the dying person will have been fraught long before he or she is actively dying, and keeping someone at home as they die will simply not be possible. Households that are tense, where difficult dynamics that pre-dated the illness have not eased up, will find it hard to cope in times like this. Like a newborn, the high needs of a dying person, the 24-hour care, will put untold stress on the family system. I have also known the most tolerant people eventually to hold their hands up and say that they can't go on responding, with intermittent professional support, in their own home;

that the burden of caring has become untenable; I have seen others wanting to take flight in the final hours, disappearing into work or onto golfing fields, as spouses move into a needier dependent state; I have witnessed carers who are desperate to keep their partners at home but who have become too ill themselves under the strain.

In these instances, the death might take place in a hospital or a hospice, and the perceived ideal good death gives way to an alternative type of death – yet sometimes death in an institution takes the pressure and tension away. Hospices often offer a space of sanctuary to families under duress; a chance for a wife to become a wife again, where gentler conversations and connections might be possible. Hospitals, too, as Seymour (2001) argues, can be sites where a good death is achieved, although it is often difficult for nurses to align the 'body work' with the 'emotional work' that is often needed around those who are dying.

Sleeping next to someone who we fear is dying is nigh on impossible, a wakeful state inevitable. For most of the remainder of the night I slept on my right hand side, watching my mother, who was now still, only the occasional twitch. It had been so harrowing to watch her body shaking, arm banging into the cream-painted wall, holding on to her so that her bones and skin did not become bruised with the force. Now it was hard to switch off my mind, and my sadness that Mum was also being battered from within by this tumour. I watched Mum breathe, an obsessional observation of the ascent and descent of her chest.

In reality there was a calmness to her breathing, yet very little calm in me. I stayed on, hoping that my presence may well have comforted her; that somehow she knew that her people would bear this final metamorphosis, that love –

that deep ability to journey with someone – was more essential than ever now. What I had picked up over the years, from being a mother, from conducting an infant observation and from caring frontline for people living with dementia, was that relationships across the life-course are vital, that we develop in relation to an-Other. Even though Mum was unconscious, there was still a relationship at play. In response to her ebbing away, to her seizures, I was discovering in myself a depth of grief that was unimaginable and yet simultaneously I was noticing a resilience that I did not believe I could possibly possess. In this desperate god-awfulness, after three nights of ongoing seizures (finally diminishing), my mother was somehow teaching me how *to be*.

Talking about infant observation methodology, Rustin (1989) highlights the mutuality of learning between mother and baby:

> [R]elationships rather than separate individuals... What is described is not merely what the baby can do, or how the baby is, but how mother and baby are developing in relationship to each other (p. 63).

Mum was un-developing, and, though I wished it to be otherwise, by being alongside her in her dying process – in the face of immense grief and pain – it was as if part of me were coming into being; a part of me that was able to stay with profound distress, an unflappable quality that she had at times demonstrated. Yet of course, in the immediacy of those moments, in the early hours of the morning, in the quiet darkness of the night, with the eventual rising of the light and the appearance of the small birds that visited her bird feeder, the thought of my own development was not consciously available. We were a family in survival.

Two days elapsed, Mum sleeping deeply, the occasional shiver in her right leg, oral midazolam fed into her cheek cavity once every few hours now, her breathing level. My father and I wandered around the house, opening and closing cupboard doors in the kitchen, and talking about how sudden this change had been. He went to the shops on occasion, collecting goodies we comforted ourselves on; I went for a run across the beautiful undulating fields all around my parents' home, searching for clarity outside where there was little inside.

It was a limbo-like existence, filled only, it seemed, with one possibility: an ending. No one ever tells you that simply sitting next to a dying person – whether you love them or not – is hard, hard work. There is an immense emotional cost to bearing witness to someone's final moments.

My husband had recognised the urgency of the situation, taking both children to France as planned for the Easter break skiing holiday. Seeing them happy and lively on the phone each day presented me with this other existence where play takes centre stage. In some way contact with them, albeit at a distance, was a yearned-for interrupting moment, an essential time to be able to forget. Even though the children seemed distracted by red runs, black runs, and bobble hats, there was a sense that they too were waiting. 'Mum,' my daughter had said, then stopping herself. 'Tell Mama we love her.' I wondered if her pause masked an unutterable question: was Mama dead yet?

Palliative care nurses and nursing assistants know the heaviness of working day in, day out, with dying people. We know, as highlighted by Hospice UK's report on Resilience (2015), that the emotional labour involved in this line of work is high. It is considered imperative, and good practice, in palliative care that workers have access to regular clinical supervision in which their feelings have an avenue for expression. In sessions such as these all across the UK, staff will talk about complex cases in the community, difficult deaths in hospices, and will be given the opportunity to reflect on those times when they are feeling flat in relation to the helplessness of supporting dying people. My father and I were beginning to experience this sense of helplessness each day – there was no Mum to feed, to talk to, to play music to. Any *doing* was replaced with *being* with her, this last experience of our small family.

Following three very long days, my mother opened her eyes. My father was with her. He shouted out. As I stooped over Mum, she blinked several times, gentle movements of the lids opening and closing – the body's way of conveying surprise. Getting her bearings from her place in the bed, only the ceiling and two peering faces from above to be seen, and there it was: that smile of Mum's that was so familiar to us all, a smile that may well have conveyed that she was here, that she was home again.

It is no understatement to say that this reawakening felt like a miracle. It is not uncommon for people – understood to be dying imminently, on the end-of-life pathway – to return, refreshed and renewed. The trajectory of dying does not always follow a straightforward linear downward path. Anselm and Glaser's (1965) sociological study of chronic illness came to see several clear patterns in dying: rapid, intermittent and gradual. Terminal conditions, or older age – or 'frailty' – tend to be gradual, though anecdotally patients and families often report the desperate unpredictability of cancer; the collapse followed by regained strength, the constant holding of breath.

Anselm and Glaser's (1965) trajectories of dying are, of course, loose conceptions since the clinical picture varies often. In hospice care, patients arrive in crisis, with a prognosis of days or hours to live; but with consistent good care, the management of pain, and perhaps a less anxiety-ridden environment, some remarkably return home. I have witnessed families preparing several times for the impending death of a mother or a father, a mixture of joy and exhaustion that comes with both extended time and a realisation that they will all have to say goodbye again. In families where this push and pull between life and death resurfaces time and time again the tensions can lead to splintering and alienation; all the ambivalent feeling towards the dying person finding targets in those that remain; the guilt in those who want to 'get back to normal'; the envious attacks on those who resist holding constant vigil.

For staff teams, too, supporting someone who keeps coming back from the brink can be emotionally exhausting, where professional prognosis seems meaningless, consultants bemused. Sometimes a patient in denial of his own death, particularly – and understandably – those who may have recuperated from illness time and time again, will have a notable impact on a hospice staff team. Curiously, a team may be drawn into that denial, and it might become difficult to disentangle the reality of a patient's condition from his or her fear to accept death. It's not uncommon for a patient's internal conflicts to find their way into the collective psyche of the team either; a patient may veer between holding out for life and simultaneously expressing a wish to die. Teams may split in two, according to the part of the patient they may meet on a given day. In cases like these, a great deal of reflection is needed to be able to hold in mind the unintegrated tensions that a person is struggling with.

On that morning when my mother opened her eyes once again, I chose to reclaim her in all her beautiful aliveness, and hoped that this would be the beginning of a long return. Though my father had abandoned his childhood indoctrination in the Church, resisting his father's path in favour of socialism, there were signs that, at some deep level, he was still a child of

God. As he held my mother's hand, stroking the white hairs on her head – some of which were detaching from her scalp and finding their way on to her red pillows – he turned to me. 'My father used to visit people who were ill, and put his healing hands on them. People got better.' His father had laid on hands, reinvigorating people. In that moment, my father too was filled, if not with religious fervour, at the very least the optimism of human life force.

It was as if my mother had come out of hibernation; there was something adorable about her emerging from this torpor, a small rodent shaking itself back into spring. Indeed it was April. I could imagine her licking her lips, shaking her head, readying herself for food. This was not far from what happened. My father, shocked yet relieved that he could now resume his caring role, went directly to the kitchen, bringing Mum water and a straw. 'Jay,' he whispered, 'would you like something to drink?'

She was desperately thirsty, drinking a glass of water and then another one. And then, more than we could have hoped for, she spoke. 'That's niiii---iii---ce,' she said.

In that moment, the tears that emerged from the back of our eyes stung with the pain of loss that had accumulated over the last few days, and at the same time a slow release of joy as it dawned on us that we may just have more time.

Time slows down when caring for someone; the speed and pace of the everyday experience seems far away. In that space, in the days alongside someone who is dying, each detail is taken in. I noticed the way Mum sucked at the straw as she took in the water, the way her toes protruded from a cover, the plumpness of her cheeks. Time was slowing because I was present in a way that took in micro-moments, micro-movements, micro-characteristics. Time was slowing because the concerns of the everyday – the high-speed chase to work, to get kids to school, to juggle tasks – were no longer part of my current reality, and my pace was attempting to mirror something of the pace of my mother's.

When people are unwell, living with a cancer or any debilitating long-term condition, there is a need (particularly as the condition progresses into its advanced stages) to be sensitive to the speed of someone's movement, of their processing, of their communications. It teaches those of us in well, able bodies and minds that time supports human relatedness at the most intimate levels when time is experienced less frenetically, when we use time to be alongside, to observe the other and ourselves in encounter together, when we just look, when we just stay. And this is not the discourse of mindfulness or meditation that I borrow from, though perhaps what I am describing is that quiet capacity of bearing witness and of taking in the phenomena of the everyday with some curiosity, but rather this is the experience of aligning ourselves with someone else's reality, demonstrating in an embodied, conscious way that you are with them as far as you are able. That, at the end of a person's life, we *are here*, prepared to join them.

> He is wheelchair-bound, hoist-dependent, medicated on gabapentin, every aspect of who he once was gradually being stripped away; where not only can he no longer move at all, but soon his swallow will go, his sight may disappear, his world shrinking into a small cramped room in his mind. He talked about once having travelled continents and taking flight; now people were leaving him. He had had plenty of friends, visitors, family, a wife, all around and physically there. But 'relationships go' he says, because his pace, his movement, his thoughts are out of sync with everyone else. He is alone.

In her eighties, she has dementia, in the midst of a busy care home, she looks around at comings and goings, relentless, 'Their world does not understand mine; mine does not understand theirs.'

To bridge the disconnect between each other's realities, at least partially, the treatment of time between the well and the unwell has to come into greater alignment; and yet this is hard to do, particularly in task-oriented organisations. But also in the private homes of dying people where the pressure of routine existence – bins out, dishwashers to stack and empty, appointments to honour – invariably forces us to pick up speed, and into doing. Long-term conditions, as the symptoms advance, almost demand an adaptation, not just of the patient but also to the informal and formal carers, to a more deeply ontological state of being, of slowing, mirroring and holding.

Certainly the weeks that followed Mum's return to consciousness were weeks that slowed down for us all. The minute-by-minute of each day was given greater attention. My father made the most beautiful meals – Mum's favourite green, green vegetables and brown, brown rice, some kind of playback to notions of healthy eating. She asked for foodstuffs in bizarre colour combinations which were not always representative of the colour things were in reality – carrots, blue; broccoli, yellow - and so we all adapted to a sort of colour-blind landscape that was hers. Dad was able to tease out the meaning of her requests, which was remarkable. It was also remarkable that, despite Mum's obvious vulnerability, she exerted such dominance over us.

I watched her eat her meals, the gratitude expressed after each bite, how delicious she found these new tastes, as if she had never experienced food before, a strange culinary reawakening;

the sound of music that teased her ears; the birds that visited in front of her window, her bed turned now to look out at the garden. All of this seen or heard for the first time.

Months ago, Mum had decided to pare down her wardrobe, and now, in the middle of April, only had a few items of her spring and summer clothes. She didn't need any of them. Bedbound, no longer able to stand to reach a commode, she could only wear large nighties that were easy for the visiting carers to slip on and off. Two nightdresses had been cut up the back with scissors, so that she could be washed on the bed with greater ease. If she were fully cognisant of these sorts of adaptations, what would she think? But it seemed now that comfort was most crucial, her proud attention to physical appearance was diminishing, though some of her appearance signatures were beginning to resurface. She still asked for a dab of mascara on her eyelashes, she was keen to be rid of a bristly chin with the electric contraption that looked more like a lipstick than a razor; the carers sprayed a little *Climat* on her wrists and on her chest. And finally she would place her glasses on, a small golden watch hanging from a chain around her neck. These signatures of external identity harked back to her days of having been the Head of an English department in several large comprehensives. This was her look, her authority, a woman once so performative and important in the corridors of school. Mum was a simulacrum of her earlier self; and no amount of perfume, mascara, jewellery would bring her back.

Mum was totally dependent on the carers from Hospice at Home, on my father and I, on the district nurses and GPs, the pharmacists, and the syringe driver that was set up to pump anti-seizure meds throughout her body. This had been set up when Mum's swallow had gone only days before.

It had been decided that the syringe driver remain in place. It was delivering medication into her left leg, made nice and cosy – at least superficially – by being placed in a handmade pale blue holdall bag with daisy white flowers. For some days Mum appeared relaxed, even enjoying the spring song and sun through the curtains, at times making an effort to participate in conversation, even finally accepting a visit from her ailing sister from whom she had hidden the truth of her predicament.

The moment came, and a short meeting by Mum's bedside took place. Between the two sisters, Mum the younger, they had managed to articulate their love for each other. It was a tender moment, and given the family history of silence I was glad that this had finally been spoken. But as my aunty continued talking, Mum began to drift off. She was elsewhere, a disconnect, that sense of slow retreat.

As my father's meals began to make my mother stronger, or so it seemed, so did her resolve to move, to make a stand. Lying prostrate in bed for several days, there came a point where she was ready to push up, to sit as upright as she could. She understood that without movement she would soil herself – despite the enormous incontinence pads she had been given – and this sense of impending indignity brought to the surface a raging soul. Mum became a force to be reckoned with – a strength of mind, withering of muscle and body. 'The wee, wee, wee,' she would shout, shaking her head violently. 'Toilet.'

Soon the frustration turned to aggression which transmuted into the wish to die. It is well documented that Freud believed that this aggression stems from a powerful *thanatos*, or the death wish, which all of us possess. Bearing with the anger of clients can be hard, particularly when the attack is overt, yet to psychically shoulder someone's aggression can be an invaluable process, offering some containment, we might hope, before dying.

And so it was that Mum – despite her seeming moments of bliss – finally reached a point of what might be described as terminal agitation. It seemed that this coincided with her realisation that she was trapped in the bed, that she would each morning wake in urine-sodden pads, that each day her body would hold on to her faeces, unable to let them go out of the shame of being cleaned. Shame had featured in Mum's childhood, and I feared it would feature in her dying days. I worried that she hated this dependent state, a return to an infantile place that awoke in her anxieties about being too much, too messy, too unlovable. In a book I had written on dementia care in the UK care home context (Ramsay-Jones, 2019), I had ended with the words:

> By hating dependency we also shame our infantile dependent self and shame ourselves as we age and move towards death. This is, quite simply, no way to go. (p. 210)

Was this some kind of premonition of my mother's death, some deeply embedded unconscious understanding of her that had become part of my script?

For three consecutive days, Mum made tragic efforts to escape the bed, to reach that small room where the toilet and the jacuzzi bath she had installed for her own mother were, but it was not to be. We had invited a physiotherapist in to see how Mum might be helped, as her upper body was undoubtedly gaining strength. I imagined a room with over-ceiling hoists, or adapted commodes, slide sheets even. But her rage was so great that Dad had called the physiotherapist to explain that the impending appointment might be best off rescheduled.

In this time, Mum protected me from her anger at still being alive, but I could see that with each failed attempt to stand her power was slipping from her. At the back of her head, her thick wiry hair had left a patch of baldness, and I remember looking at it, relieved at least that she could not see it. In the nightie, with the back cut – a sort of cape – she pushed herself up to sitting, me holding on to her back and willing myself to be able to raise her so that she would have enough purchase to push up and place her feet to the floor. We struggled together, wishing for a combined strength that would allow Mum the experience of being vertical once again. Her body was giving up. She could no longer hold herself upright, even seated for long. She waited for some minutes, her arms around my small body and mine around hers, as if in the waiting she might simply find the fuel to push down and stand. Her feet were dangling over the side of the bed, her legs bloated with fluid. Her toes looked twisted, though her toenails themselves were neat and recently cut by a visiting pedicurist.

I remembered my days in care homes, the older women who needed hoisting to commodes, who needed careful handling, a constant vocal reminder of each movement, in the extremity of their dependency. Now here I was with my mother, keeping hold of her back and trying desperately to keep hold of her identity. 'Mum, perhaps we can try a frame and use the commode,' I had said, unrealistically, drawn into Mum's determination to get up. I called out to my father, who made it clear that this time, my optimism was misguided. He reminded me of the awful falls that would no doubt haunt him in his grief.

We retried a few times a day for several days; yet the furthest we got was to the end of the bed, holding each other, upright, but with fallen heads, foreheads pressed together, a recognition between us that this was the final struggle. We cannot rescue people in life, neither can we rescue people from death's inevitability. Sometimes we feel as if we are failing people, by asking them to rest back down; it is immensely painful to see a person defeated and unravelling. Mum was now ready, readier than she had ever been, to die.

She would bring out her smile, for us, followed swiftly and firmly by, 'Die, die, die, I want to die.' Tension was everywhere, most prominently held in her physical body. She became severely constipated. She would not shit her bed and create more mess than she was already creating; the control was tight and unwavering. Yet in this holding on, and holding in, the pain became greater. With incredible skill and sensitivity, the district nurses managed to help her, but it was not without its agony for my father, who had lived with a proud, clean and in control woman all his life.

At this point Mum was still eating dad's experimental vegan dinners, small bowls of noodles and brown rice, and drinking hot chocolate two to three times a day. It seemed that there might be a possibility that she would rally further. Dad's care was all in the detail: the way he worked out exactly what Mum would wish to eat – the number of broccoli florets, the colours in the bowl and in her mind, the straw in the hot chocolate, the curtains opened at a certain time when she was fully awake. All in the finest detail.

Erich Fromm (1942) asks in *The Fear of Freedom* the question, 'Why is spontaneous activity the answer to the problem of freedom?' It may be a tangential link but, working with people who are dying, this question sometimes becomes part of the story.

Psychotherapy in general is about the human story, reworking and re-scripting it; it is – as the days and sessions go on – also about love and loveableness; can it be found and be inhabited with some sense of security? One way into personal freedom, which paradoxically allows us to feel secure, is through acts of spontaneity – a spontaneity which communicates the full expression of the self.

Fromm's book is brilliant because his notion of the self, of individualism, is not the empty shell of the individual constructed through capitalist discourse, the hungry ghost looking for sustenance in endless external commodity. But an individual that, through development and growth, rediscovers and recognises that his individualism is predicated on linking and on a sense of relatedness with other men and with nature.

When I hear of those who spontaneously fill the gaps of need for their terminally ill and fatigued partners who can no longer do the dishwasher, wash the clothes, do the food shop, take the photos, fill the memory boxes, remember the songs, it becomes clear that some of the most liberating spontaneous activities are those small gestures which, quite simply, free us as individual human beings through dynamic acts of love, and through our affirmation – in the everydayness of existence – of others. I kept thinking about Dad's role, and how there was both routine and spontaneity involved: the routine held him together; the spontaneity was in the constant adaptation to Mum's state of mind and need.

Now, back home, our children had returned from their trip. Mum had understood this to be the case. I sat on the side of her bed, holding a glass of water, placing a straw in her mouth to ease any dryness. She looked at me, smiling, that sweet smile, a childlike innocence and naivety communicated in it, which was still there despite her age and predicament. 'Go home,' she said, 'love, love, love, to your babies.'

How do some mothers continue to mother till the end like this? I was reminded of the book *Wild*, Cheryl Strayed's story of personal discovery and travel after being orphaned at twenty-six; I thought of her mother's words, uttered in debilitating weakness:

'Love,' she whispered, too weak to say the *I* and *you*.
'Love,' she said again as I left the room. (p. 25)

This maternal love would also be part of my inheritance – a message about the value of life and of my own children, of care and concern. Facing her own endpoint, she could still go beyond herself to the continuation of the generation to come – the most generous offering that a dying mother could give.

These were her last ever words to me. That final sentence holds within it a deep realisation of the wider set of responsibilities we have to one another; the words from a mother to a daughter, a mother to a mother. She was allowing herself to withdraw into the shadows, making way for the unfurling of those younger. Mum would leave with love.

Though we know that many of us have this sense of unconditional love available to us, this expansiveness, somehow it always takes us by surprise, it moves us.

He will die two days from now. Despite, or perhaps because of her profession, she bends down and gently kisses his forehead. He looks up, eyes yellow with jaundice, stomach distended, protruding through the sheets, and he manages to smile at her, a smile that lingers and holds her there; a thank you, a quiet act of gratitude to be cherished. She takes her leave, experiencing the sadness of saying goodbye, and yet the sheer wonderment at this man's generosity in dying stays with her. Perhaps this brief moment tells us what love looks like.

My father-in-law, one week before he died of an aggressive cancer of unknown origin – living only six weeks from initial diagnosis – had struggled over to the local park, supported by his son, my husband, to see our children kick a ball around. He was weak, tired, days later he would lose his eyesight. The stamina and strength he had summoned up that day stays with me: my son, nearly three, held in his hand a small plastic helicopter toy that his grandfather had given him that morning. One of its components had snapped. My son took it to Tom, explained that the toy could no longer fly. Ever the fixer, my father-in-law stood on, shaking in the cold, making sure his grandson would have something whole to remember him by. The toy mended, Fearghas had reached up as small children do, wanting a pick-up, a cuddle from this man, who had seen his need and responded to it. Tom had bent down, I simply don't know how, and held Fearghas tight to his own body and attempted to walk both of them back home. He could only manage metres, until he had to hand Fearghas to his dad. Sometimes we say of human moments and the gifts we give, *it was the thought that counts.* When I look back on those short, yet expansive, minutes, the final time our children saw their grandfather, it becomes clear that *it is the thought and it is the action* and *it is always the love which drives both that counts.*

Intellectually, we may know that:

> Death, which will strike our loved ones and our friends, is perhaps what pushes us not to be content with living on the surface of things and people, pushes us to enter into the heart and depth of them. (Marie de Hennezel, 1997, p. xii)

As professionals we are touched by death and dying people: we learn from them; we see that the heart of many dying people is open. Indeed my mother's communication of love and responsibility to the *babies* continues to be an internal reference point for me. In grief, on difficult days I will hark back to her words and also those of de Hennezel, which remind us: 'Don't pass by life; don't pass by love' (Marie de Hennezel, 1997, p. xiv).

We might be able to imagine the experience of a son or a daughter leaving his or her parent on a hospital bed, in a terminal condition, and driving the hour and a half down the motorway. It physically hurts. There is a dull aching pressure in the chest, tears build up in the back of the eyes as you drive away. There is both focus on the journey, a desire to get back to some semblance of normality, and no focus at all. I could see the motorway and see the road but it seemed to have no meaning to me. All it signified was a movement away from my mother and yet simultaneously she had gone nowhere. The car rushed past fields on the left and right, and took a forward-bound trajectory yet I was still in the room with her and seeing her smile over and over again. To think that someone could smile as they lie dying is something that my mind cannot grasp; that gentle command to be alright, to continue to mother, in the midst of a family's fragmentation. 'Go to your babies.' Over and over again, I heard her.

Mothers, when all is going well, can be secure bases (Bowlby, 1979) from which their children explore the world, depart and come back, depart and come back. She was showing me that, even in the most insecure of times, in death, she would be a secure enough base from which I could depart and continue my life; to return to being that secure enough base to my own children. The anxious thought that she may have been hiding any fear or sadness so I could take leave still plagues me at times: the residual what ifs, the bargainings, the constant ruminations of grief.

Denise Riley (2019) in her deeply tender, incisive essay on grief talks about time being arrested in the aftermath of her son's death. To lose a child at any point, suddenly, must empty a mother out, and it was true that I still had my children. But there was a temporal and spatial disruption going on in those weeks and days before my mother died that reminded me of the weeks after my children were born: a suspension, a constant focus on the most intricate movements and details, the closing and shutting out of petty concerns, the inability to follow unfolding conversation as if it were devoid of sense; the awareness of subjectivity itself interrupted and morphing, pulled and stretched in different directions.

I stopped at a petrol station on the way home, filled up, and left. Weeks later I received a letter, explaining that I had not paid for the tank of petrol and could I do so. Disconnected from these everyday concerns, at times it was as if I had become unanchored from the pragmatic realities of the material world.

I passed my turn-off and kept driving, reaching Evesham and then doubling back once I had realised that I had driven miles beyond the turn-off to the M4. My concentration was shot to pieces, a shell-like pilot, a driverless car. When I found myself back on a country road, the road I had driven along to take my mother to her radiotherapy sessions, I stopped. I pulled over, staring at the most golden field of rapeseed flowers and shamrock green grasses and an intensely turquoise spring sky. I climbed the gate to take in the scene, and imagined that my mother, once dead, would one day be part of this vast resonance field of existence and of life and death. We have to imagine the dead somewhere and this is where I would place her. Here, among nature's colours, and by her mulberry tree.

Would my mother have a good death if I were not there? What would constitute one for her – alone but at home?

Surrounded by family? Free from pain? Often I have spoken to colleagues about our ideas of the good death: even those accustomed to seeing many many deaths, those at the frontline of nursing care, have reservations about its meaning. Who, after all, is this good death for – a good death for the patient, or the family, or as judged by society, impacted as it is with normativising discourses of control and manageability? Not all deaths can be demonstrated as good or as bad. As Gleckman (2019) points out:

> What's troubling about this drive for a good death… is that many of us never will achieve it – often for reasons out of our control. And that may leave our surviving loved ones with an even bigger sense of guilt than they already have. And paradoxically, those who cared the most may end up feeling the most guilty and depressed. Failing at some ideal of death may even make dying more difficult… The idea of competitive dying may be counterproductive in part because there is no true good death. Or rather there are millions of them… And researchers have no real idea how many people do in fact die a good death, by whatever measure. (Gleckman, Forbes, July 2019)

With all of this in mind, I worried that my mother was trying her hardest to live up to this idea of a good death, and that that was an extra burden on her, but I had to let go of these thoughts because when I studied her facial expressions, her bodily gestures, they aligned with her words – that she was indeed accepting of her end and was increasingly tired of being unwell. No longer was her terminal agitation and fury still present. She seemed to be reaching a peaceful state, the preparation to leave.

In the aftermath of her death, my father found a note buried in Mum's shoe, a sort of grounding message – the fundamentals of who she came to be. On it, she had written:

1. Slim

2. Painlessness

3. Flexibility

4. Live to 85

5. Live long enough for those I love

So it stands to reason that when Mum heard that she had an aggressive glioblastoma her first thoughts were towards life. Death, ultimately, was never going to be a good experience. When Dad told me about this note, what became more striking over the four months of living with cancer was the way Mum had adapted to the reality that she was dying, with a courage and dignity I simply didn't expect.

The morning after I had returned home to see the children, my father called. He was sure that Mum was dying; again, she would not be roused. I would return home.

It seems increasingly that we are collectively able to think about death, and cultural trends bear this out. But what about the dying part, the messier, more disturbing process that we all have to go through? This does not involve the neatness of choosing headstones and floral displays: it's about states of mind and disintegrating bodies. What might a good dying entail? For my mother, as for the many people with terminal illnesses, the process of dying starts long before they are considered end-of-life: dying becomes part of the psychic world, revisited and reconsidered time and time again. Preparations are made to leave the world, and often to leave it behind without creating too much work for those who remain. Yet this must be an inordinately difficult act: for how can we imagine ourselves absent while still alive, functioning in the day-to-day of existence.

The moment you start to write yourself out of the script of other people's lives, a whole host of powerful feelings take hold. People move to being numb, disengaged, withdrawn, unable to participate; ordinary participation no longer has the same meaning, as if a dying person is already one removed: does the dishwasher matter, now, a clean pair of socks, Meghan and Harry's exit, the Brexit shambles? Sometimes I notice that people distract themselves with small talk, it seems a necessary footing among others; but many dying people also develop a deep sense of existential awareness, the colour of flowers and leaves, the sweetness of children and the closeness of ties – that sense of being part and yet apart. And of course there is also the mess, the anger, envy, the desire to die quickly and fast, to avoid the slow demise, the prolonged goodbyes. Some are able to be generous, in this liminal space, others not so. In her novel, *Sight*, Jessie Greengrass's narrator talks of her mother:

> *A decision had been made, somewhere in the closing corridors of her mind: that she would no longer try to reach beyond herself, nor put aside the business of dying in favour of an experience she had no way of holding on to. She could have been generous. I might have liked to have, later on, this memory of sitting with her watching sunlight fall on water, a last fragment of accord, but she had nothing left to give me now, not even this.*
> (Greengrass, 2018, p. 19)

So a good dying is perhaps about being able to find others with whom all those experiences can be shared, and that's really as good as it can get: a sense that one's aloneness in death is recognised as just that, a uniquely human process, yet can become a shared collective responsibility.

As I arrived home on the morning of my father's phone call, I could see the cars of the Hospice at Home team, who had got to know Mum for the last month and whose patient, genuine care was always welcomed. She loved being freshened up, the chattiness she would try to follow, the way the men and women tended to those appearance signatures. But now she was unconscious, no more sound.

Two of the carers heard me come into the room, and explained as sensitively as they could that Mum wasn't responding. We had said goodbye two days before. Now only I was saying hello, but she heard me; somewhere in all that cut-offness I was still recognised as one of her someones. She opened her eyes, sticky with hours of closure. She smiled at me. A hello and goodbye together. She returned to sleep.

The thing about dying for those bearing witness, who are waiting, is that there are variations of death and endings. The changes are slow to begin with, incremental losses, small changes, small deaths, and then they pick up pace until there is no more. The Buddhists say we are born again each minute, and yet those micro-shifts are imperceptible to the outside; only we know our thoughts are ebbing and flowing in response to our contextual existence; on the inside we see that our feelings never remain constant and can transmute from sadness to joy, anger to empathy. But in a long-term condition, we see the change also on the outside, a change that will culminate in death – a death of who and what we have known relationally, and a birth into an ever-absence that brings someone back strangely in newly understood ways.

A calm descended in our home, as we sensed that Mum

was dying. The district nurses gave us the leaflet about what to expect of someone's breathing. This was a telling sign, the information about the final moments; the GP visited, empathetic, considered, noting our tiredness and also our pain; Mum was handled with such tenderness by the care team; and my father and I sat around her bed at different times. We slept next to her at night; and took short breaks in the day. For two nights, we barely slept as her breathing had become so deep, so loud, so oppressive in the darkened room. End-stage respiratory secretions, or the 'death rattle', is said to occur in some patients when they become weaker or lose consciousness, with a median time from onset of the rattle until death between 11 and 24 hours.

With this knowledge, and the sound emanating from Mum, it was hard to hold on to any internal serenity, and yet this was the kind of resilience that a dying person might need of his or her people; an ability to go inwards to find a moment's peace, the capacity to know when a temporary departure from the enclosure of death was necessary to be able to go back and sit, hand in hand, again.

Time seemed to simultaneously stretch and shorten. The sheer waiting was exhausting, yet the thought of wishing this time away left a jarring sense of guilt. As Greengrass (2018) writes:

> ... my tearful fervour the result of a denial, not of how close my mother was to death, how it shivered about us, a long boundary to be crossed, but of how I wished it would be done because I was exhausted and because there was nothing I could do now but sit and watch, and even that was too much. (p.19)

On the day that my mother died, I knew instinctively that I could not leave her. Next to her, stroking her silvery hair, reading a book, holding her hand. Soon that breathing came, the loud booming, rattling breath that pointed to the end. It was as if the walls were coming in on me, that her breath was volcanic, no way out of this final eruption.

We had been told, as many families learn, that hearing would be the last thing to go for Mum. And so I began to read my mother's favourite poem, Louis MacNeice's 'Sunlight on the Garden', the one she wanted us to sprinkle her ashes to. What was this live funeral I was giving her, as she rattled and spat out thick yellowy secretions that I wiped from the side of her mouth? On one level, here was a macabre ghoulish scene, yet on another I wanted some beauty to intervene; that love of poetry, of words, that had seemingly woven itself into the fabric of her being as a young girl who had tried to find respite from the ugliness of her formative years, the poverty and upending chaos of an unreliable father. Go out in beauty, Mum.

> *The sunlight on the garden*
> *Hardens and grows cold.*
> *We cannot cage the minute*
> *Within its nets of gold;*
> *When all is told*
> *We cannot beg for pardon.*
>
> *Our freedom as free lances*
> *Advances towards its end;*
> *The earth compels, upon it*
> *Sonnets and birds descend;*
> *And soon, my friend,*
> *We shall have no time for dances.*

The sky was good for flying
Defying the church bells
And every evil iron
Siren and what it tells:
The earth compels,
We are dying, Egypt, dying

And not expecting pardon,
Hardened in heart anew,
But glad to have sat under
Thunder and rain with you,
And grateful too
For sunlight on the garden.

As I read to her, I could see a tear emerge, streaming from her right eye, and it seemed that this was yet another one of her poignant goodbyes. We convince ourselves of all sorts of things in our lifetimes; we also convince ourselves that we are wrong. We tell ourselves that white feathers can't possibly be the symbols of the dead person's spirit, or that the appearances of robins around the dying is nothing but a reassuring fiction. And yet here I am, often rationally minded like the rest of us, and now I simply do not know. Her tears were speaking, though, I have little doubt, of one final sadness that she would not hear the tender exactitude of these words again, or the sound of her daughter's voice. In under an hour, with a few final deep and laboured bouts of breathing and a thickness of her respiratory secretions that the district nurse had tried her best to quell with an additional round of scopolamine, my mother's breathing became quieter and lighter.

'Dad,' I called, attempting to contain any signs of panic. And there we were all three letting each other go until Mum became silence.

And then the silence comes
Breath extinguished
Life flowing into endless expanse
Strangely beautiful. For now.

Absence and Grief

'It's as if, from a set of nested Russian wooden dolls, the
innermost ones had fallen out.'

DENISE RILEY (2019)

'We may be rational creatures, deeply individual, but loss
illuminates just how readily the ever-uncertain fortress of
reason crumbles, and how fundamentally our individuality
is made up of our attachments to others.'

LISA APPIGNANESI (2018)

Today is the first birthday I will have without my mother; without her input; a telephone call, a scrawled card – for she was not a pedantically neat hand-writer – a wintery jumper, hand-knit, vibrant. Sadness descends on a day like today, right from the moment of waking, and it is hard to shake. You feel thinned out, papery, grief barely disguised by cheery skins that we, the bereaved, often wrap ourselves up with.

When someone we have often talked to, and discussed our life events with, dies, we frequently wish we could hear their voice again, if only for a moment. Many of us who are grieving might regret not having kept some sort of video in which they are chatting; the sound of an answerphone, for instance, as a reminder of how he or she sounded.

There are two forms of voice, perhaps, the external voice – the tone, the timbre, the inflections, and the one or two sweet words, or catchphrases, that might have formed part of their daily speech. And there is an internal voice – the one that the bereaved person carries in their mind, the life lessons, the wisdom, left, which perhaps takes on added meaning in the aftermath of someone's death. (Of course, for some, the voice might be more difficult, accusatory, harsh – which, with support, might over time be understood in a different way, we can only hope).

And while I have an internal voice to draw from today, there is nothing like hearing your Mum call up on your birthday – a day symbolising umbilical connection and disconnection.

Though there is joy to be found this morning, particularly in the buoyancy of our children who have written birthday cards to me – our daughter ever comedic, our son a sometimes sensitive poetic sort in the making – there is a notable absence today. It is now for me a moment to pause and reflect, to give some space to the huge influence my mother's life has had on me: as an art student, putting together portfolios for my GCSEs, I had reworked another Louis MacNeice poem, 'A Prayer Before Birth'. It was Mum who will have shown it to me. It had resonated deeply with me, that experience of voicelessness, of being unheard.

The drama of my own birth had been told and retold so many times: Mum had nearly died, me too; her caesarean scar had become infected, breastfeeding was hard owing to the pain of the gaping wound, yet she had persevered with gritty determination and heightened anxiety. In my mind, I always imagined having been fed too much, such was the level of her anxiety, and other more complex newborn communications might have been misrecognised in her state of panic; whatever it was, those early primordial pre-verbal times were, I sensed, filled with unease. For the art exam, I had painted a giant watercolour, an '80s version of Titian's Madonna and Child, c. 1540, with a mother cradling a baby. The mother's fingernails were a ruby red, spoiling the image of innocence: those nails are overbearing in the image, as my own real and internal mother had also been as I grew up. To run alongside MacNeice's poem, I had constructed a floating womb-space, made with bamboo and netting – inside, a small felt baby not yet born. The story of my birth had been a haunting, and my dominant mother had at times silenced me in the fullness of my own developing voice.

But here I am – many years later and having reconciled our difficulties, separations and returns – being born again, without her. Grief gives birth to an expression of the self that can be discombobulating, particularly for those who have repressed, during their life-course, their own emotional repertoire. All these bewildering feelings can make people believe they are going mad. Being a psychotherapist, having scripted and re-scripted my feelings about the events of my life has, I believe, given me tools to understand my own grief, to feel less shocked by its impact, and the power of feelings therein. For bereaved people who may exist in more tightly controlled emotional states – storing feelings away in the bowels of the unconscious – the leaking of feeling, the eruption of sadness, anger, confusion, the immensity of gratitude, can cause panic and a sense of interior chaos, particularly when they realise that now there is limited capacity to control such feelings from bursting through the surface at inopportune times. As Julia Samuel (2017), in her wonderful book, *Grief Works*, writes:

> I have regularly seen that it is not the pain of grief that damages individuals... and even whole families, sometimes for generations, but the things they do to avoid pain. (p. xiii)

Grief and unresolved mourning, it seemed, had been part of the transgenerational trauma imparted to my own mother through the silences of my grandmother, and the violences of my grandfather, following the sudden death of her eldest brother. A family shrouded in pain, unspoken, unprocessed, meant that Mum – at least when I was growing up – experienced a constant fear of loss, playing out with me in her panicked and often adhesive attachment to me.

My father, also a silent man, whose intellect has frequently guarded him against the onslaught of his emotional world, will tell me time and time again now that he is taken aback continually by the guilt, regret, sadness that his days are sometimes punctured by. But at least he talks. He is curious, it seems, about why he now cries at adverts for cancer research whereas before he would have batted it off without a second thought; he rereads Mum's poems and goes in search of meaning; he sees the spices in the cupboard that she collected her whole life and wishes she was there to tell him off about overusing the chilli or paprika. This is grief. As Riley (2019) says, it is 'time without its flow'.

Grief is also a dynamic active process, following the rupture of attachments we have made over the life-course. Any real or perceived threats to such bonds can induce, among other feelings, anxiety, fear, panic. When an attachment figure withdraws, as Bowlby would testify, withdrawal and despair can ensue. Murray Parkes (2010), who worked with Bowlby, writing on bereavement and attachment, likens this to the baby's relationship to the face of its caregivers:

> It has been shown experimentally that a baby's propensity to smile at a human face will gradually disappear if the human face consistently fails to smile back. (p. 13)

It might follow, then, that the smiling face of grievers is regularly masking an experience of withdrawal and sadness.

Stroebe & Schut (1995/6), psychologists writing from a more scientific perspective, conducted research into how people cope with a death, with bereavement. What they found is that people tend to need to confront their grief head on and simultaneously avoid it: there are sequences of oscillation in the grieving process. Most people will testify to these shifting states, from focusing on the absence and the loss – looking at photographs, rereading notes – and hiding away from it – becoming busy, running, returning to routine and so forth. But whether grief is finally absent, as Kubler-Ross's (1969) stage or Worden's (1991) task model might imply, is quite another question. The idea of letting go is perhaps too simplified an understanding. Klaser's (1996) continuing bonds – a less Eurocentric, sociological frame – seem to be more applicable. While the initial shock, an agonising splintering of certainty, the acuteness of those earlier months of missing, might subside, bereaved people often report an adjusted state of existence, where the gaps someone has left cannot be filled, that grief is always just beneath the surface, that pain becomes a more easily accessible part of their lives. Increasingly, too, those writing on grief (Aragno, 2003; Riley, 2019; Light, 2019) suggest that this should be so: that grief provides space for the continuation of a love that we, the bereaved, do not wish to tire of.

The moment Mum died, a silence descended in the study that was both light and heavy. I began to comfort myself with the idea that Mum had simply left her body, and was now part of the cosmos. In his much lauded book, *The Denial of Death*, Ernest Becker talks of the notion of 'cosmic specialness', a sort of residual trace of infantile primary narcissism, our desire to be noticed and to be recognised as unique. He suggests that through adulthood we engage in a mythical heroic system in the West, building up our bank balances and reaching to the heights of our careers in order to replicate, or to seek out, something of the special place we may have held, or failed to hold, as small dependent creatures in the eyes of our parents. For me, it seemed as if – in that moment – in death Mum had achieved this cosmic specialness: not only had her breath become part of the room, and further outwards into the surrounding valley and air, but she had died in love and with love.

Though of course the impact of Mum's death has changed over time, in that immediate moment or hour or day after she died, having been with her at the end of her life, having sat with her, her hand in mine, uttering the words that I had carried in my heart, as she spluttered out of existence and into calm, I felt nothing but a strange sense of relief and joy. In the foreword to Becker's *The Denial of Death*, Sam Keen writes of Ernest's courage as he faced his own death, 'It is a privilege to have witnessed such a man in the heroic agony of his dying.' In some ways, the word privilege is such a fitting one to describe my experience of Mum's death, and I only hope she too knew that she was surrounded with love.

Sometimes in my work as a psychotherapist in palliative care, I hear of people having had similar experiences. This does not minimise the pain that a death of someone we love evokes; some people will be inconsolable for many months, if not years. The way someone dies often has an impact on the nature of the grief: one which is or is not undercut with trauma; hatred or love. As Murray-Parkes and Prigerson (2010) point out, 'Problems in loving commonly give rise to problems in grieving.' This stands to reason since the absence of love in our earliest years gives rise throughout the life-course to insecurity, ambivalence and attachment difficulties. Why would a partner or parent's death, where the relationship was perpetually tense or unkind, not generate the same disorganised, overwhelmed – or conversely rigid, controlled, avoidant – response in grief?

On the other hand, while still in pain, there are people who speak of the dead with gratitude, a gratitude that has a different quality to the kind of idealisation that may cover up more aggressive impulses. One woman I had heard about, who had lost her sister abruptly to cancer, spoke of the way that her sister had generated forms of sociability maintained in love all of her life, and this was given back to her in death. Like all those in the community of the bereaved, she seemed implicitly aware that:

> The pain of grief is just as much a part of life as the joy of love: it is, perhaps, the price we pay for love, the cost of commitment. (Murray Parkes & Prigerson, 2010, p. 6)

Mum's body lay on the hospital bed; she was not yet cold to touch. She looked like her mother, who always seemed to be at rest, in the later years of her life. Mum's eyes were closed, her head resting on a terracotta pillow – no tension in her face. Somehow this was soothing. There are of course deaths which do not symbolise a peaceful departure, and on occasion dying people leave writhing in pain or their lives are shockingly cut off. Dignity in Dying's *The Inescapable Truth* (2019) report is testament to this. We know that there is little soothing memory for the bereaved in circumstances such as these. When the endings are traumatic, or untimely, people can enter into profound states of functional and emotional impairment in daily life, with intense enduring symptoms that can persist over long periods.

Freud, developing his thinking in *On Murder, Mourning and Melancholia* back in 1917, made a distinction between the mental features of mourning and those of melancholia. While he saw that both mourning and melancholia were reactions to the loss of a loved object, melancholia had a quality more akin to what we might – in current parlance – describe as complicated grief. Freud described the characteristics of melancholia as:

> a profoundly painful dejection, cessation of interest in the outside world, loss of the capacity to love, inhibition of all activity, and a lowering of self-regarding feelings to a degree that finds utterances in self-reproaches and self-revilings, and culminates in a delusional expectation of punishment. (p. 244)

He went on to make one final crucial point:

> In mourning it is the world which has become poor and empty; in melancholia it is the ego itself. (p. 246)

In more contemporary language, then, what Freud suggests is that in melancholia the former libidinal love object/person, towards whom ambivalence was once directed and who '*should have*' been loved, becomes enmeshed with the ego itself and yet splits from it, transforming into a denigrating and depleting force which attacks the ego as object itself. In normal mourning, Freud argues, there is a conscious sense of loss of the whole object, the capacity for missing a full human person; we might imagine that in melancholia all the hatred once felt, yet repressed, towards the now lost object turns back in on the grieving person in a prolonged self-attack. The lost object is idealised, beyond reproach, protected from the bereaved's unrelenting anger.

Katherine Shear, an American psychiatrist, taking a more pragmatic approach, has more recently argued that some people are so stunned by grief that they need help in the form of anti-depressant or anti-anxiety medication and/or psychotherapy. Her work has shown that returning to the actual site of death through storytelling and replay, sometimes repeatedly, can help with the symptoms of distress. Again this says something about the paradox that we can only effectively avoid something when we begin to look at and think about it. Yet, as Joan Didion passionately writes in *The Year of Magical Thinking* (2012), she is critical, irrationally angry – she says – towards a Dr Volkan of the University of Virginia who proposes 're-grief therapy' and the push to review the circumstances of a death as a way of treating 'pathological mourners'. She says:

> Unusual dependency (is that a way of saying 'marriage'? 'husband and wife'? 'mother and child'? 'nuclear family'?) is not the only situation in which complicated or pathological grief can occur. (Didion, p. 54)

She goes on indirectly to list memories, one after the other, of her deceased husband as a way of demonstrating that all grievers will attempt to keep 'the lost one' alive.

Indeed, in academic circles, there is some disagreement about the medicalisation of bereavement. For instance, Astrid James (2012) of the medical journal *The Lancet*, stated that:

> feelings of deep sadness, loss, sleeplessness, crying, inability to concentrate, tiredness, and no appetite, after the death of a loved one, could be diagnosed as depression, rather than as a normal grief reaction...

Grief is not an illness, it is more usefully thought of as a
part of being human and a normal response to the death
of a loved one. (p. 589)

These remarks had followed the American Psychiatric
Association's proposal to add grief reactions to their list of
mental illnesses in the *Diagnostic and Statistical Manual of Mental
Disorders*, otherwise known as the DSM-V (APA, 2013).

Nonetheless for my father and I there was a sense that we
were, in relation at least to the way that Mum had died and
been cared for, among the lucky ones. Lucky is not a word that
can readily be associated with death because, as a good friend
once said to me, 'death is shit'. When we love someone, there is
no real upside to losing them. Though narratives abound about
the learning and growth that can be done following someone's
death, that capacity – for instance to reclaim parts of the self
that may have been disavowed in self, and located in the dead
other – to transform through grief exists, but this is far from the
conscious mind in the weeks and months after someone dies.

The death of someone we love leaves us with a hole in our
lives, one which can't be filled with substitutes – whether people,
experiences, objects, food or drink, which may momentarily
at least give us a break from the mourning work. As Dr Lois
Tonkin, in her model *Growing Around Grief* (1996), points out,
that hole does not necessarily diminish with time but rather
life begins to sprout up around that hole, fresh and eventually
invigorating.

But there is more to it than that, and this, as I have already
proposed, has to do with the love that is left over from that
relationship and which is stored deep inside us. The reason why
the death of someone who has been valuable to us is so painful,
perhaps, is that the love which we carried in our hearts for

them no longer has a focus in actual material reality. Yes, it is internalised, and yes we can imagine memories with fondness; we can hear their voices tentatively guiding us; we can see their faces and smile to ourselves quietly. But ultimately we cannot make offerings in daily life that will bring a smile to theirs; no more cups of tea in the morning, jokes to be shared, gifts to send, meaningful conversations to be had or trips to unwind together on... And so there is a question, what do we do with this huge reserve of love? Working with grieving people, I often notice a point in the therapeutic process where a person, reflecting on his own life, and identity, starts to review where he is at as an individual in relation to others, to his work, to his own values. And cautiously he might suggest that he is ready to walk a new path. American psychologist, Abraham Maslow, who greatly influenced Carl Rogers, talked of the notion of self-actualisation, when a person's ideal self becomes congruent with his day-to-day behaviour: on the surface this sounds purely self-gratifying, outside the realms of the social. And though I know little about humanistic approaches, both men in fact took up a holistic phenomenological approach to human beings, noting that we are all beings-in-the-world alongside others, never in isolation.

This is not to associate grief easily with the possibility of change – in psychotherapy this can be a protracted, difficult process – as I have already said, because, for those of us who mourn, the pain can be searing. However, and this is crucial, there is something about working with the reserve of love, and resignifying the inevitable ambivalent feeling too, that can take us places: we can of course use this love to cloak ourselves, which is important in terms of self-care. But we can also use it in the service of our wider society. So it is not surprising, then, that many grieving people choose a different track in life – unfulfilling jobs, for instance, are abandoned in favour of more prosocial roles; relationships with existing family and friends might start to deepen; and creative endeavours, perhaps long stalled, are taken up. That remaining love, once directed towards the person now gone, becomes a love reconstructed and redirected into a raft of meaningful, compassionate choices.

It is this understanding that I take forward each day. For me, succumbing to the deadening pull of grief is neither desired nor an option. Life is here before me, worth taking up. And yet there is something strange that happens in the period of mourning, as if time has altered itself. Denise Riley (2019), again, unflinchingly describes the way she continues to exist in a state of arrested time, exploring the texture of a relationship remade between those who remain and those no longer. She says of each day without her child: 'it's a temporality of love – if the affection between the living and the now dead had been strong enough.'

For me, in the weeks and early months that followed Mum's death, linear time – the routine of my everyday – was punctured with a numbing, otherworldly suspension. It was a sense of my own time belonging to someone else, even though of course that someone else was dead. Yet of course Mum had died as an older woman, who had lived a life that was on the whole a good one, as she had said, a meaningful one. I had not lost a child, as Riley had, a separation that must find its way into the crevices of every part of you; a relentless ache and emptiness, where time hovers rather than moves. Nonetheless, grief for all of us perhaps does unusual things with time, which is most noticeable when we allow ourselves to slow down.

Early on the most striking quality of my own grief was the level of confusion I felt, as if my brain too was growing a baffling tumour. I felt permanently bewildered which morphed into a residual anxiety: each day I worried that I would not find myself under more strain, more collapse. I worried that I was rushing myself into full functioning; worried that Mum's death had not had more of an impact; worried about my children and the impact of the empty space Mum had left in their lives; worried that I wouldn't be able to work with clients who had brain tumours. But what confused and worried me most was a sense that I was relatively stable in grief. This is where the anxiety resided; despite my close relationship with Mum, I feared it wasn't real. C S Lewis (1961) wrote, 'No one ever told me that grief felt so like fear. I am not afraid, but the sensation is like being afraid.' Why wasn't I breaking or broken? This voice in my mind, which I could hear loudly at times, was in counterpoint to another, that she had given me the gift of a secure attachment in her death and so somehow I was bound to be alright.

At times I woke at night, the interrupted sleep mirroring the interruption that had taken place in our lives. I worried at night that Mum had been frightened but didn't want to worry us, that we had let her go too stoically, that we hadn't fought the cancer battle as others claimed they had… It was all around, this confusion. Eventually, speaking to a colleague informally in the corridor, I decided to allow myself the confusion, and to try to understand it.

There it was: I was confused that my mother, who, in my earliest years, had wanted to control almost my every move and guide me through life based on her own fears, losses and preoccupations for material stability, a sort of narcissistic, though loved, object or enterprise of a daughter, had died without expressing a shed of narcissism. I was confused because we had lost a whole woman in the end, a very whole woman, and she had lost a whole daughter and husband. Parting whole is somehow, though, at least for me, so much more manageable in the long run than partings between half-formed objects.

When I looked at Mum's body that day, I understood that she had lived a whole life. As Helen Nearing writes in her preface to *Light on Aging and Dying* (1995):

> The whole of our lives so far has been our message... We can deepen our awareness; we can fulfil ourselves and help others by imparting what we may have learned from the high and low phases of our existence. In that way we may find completion at the end of our lives... (p. viii)

After a few hours, the district nurses who had looked after Mum came to sign the paperwork stating that she had died. Both women had got to know her, and she had shared with them her plans to have her ashes sprinkled by the mulberry tree. In a wonderful treatise on 'The Value of Death', Ros Taylor (2019) cites Charles Leadbeater in the DEMOS Report, who describes a good death as being partially predicated on:

> Dying in the presence of people who know how to drop the professional role mask and relate to others simply and richly as human beings.

What Mum had found in the district nurses and the nursing assistants from Hospice at Home was just that: basic decent humanity, seamlessly incorporated into the tasks of professional duty.

On that day when Mum's body waited to be taken by the funeral directors, the district nurses had spoken to Mum, knowing there would be no answer, and explained to her now-body-only that she looked so very at peace, which in fact she did. They asked Dad and me if they could dress her, and at first we were reluctant, as if to query whether Mum would want to be moved now. But she was wearing a cut-up-the-back nightie and there seemed to be an indignity in leaving her like this: after all, thinking cross-culturally, the Tana Torajans (Doughty, 2017), who meticulously clean the bones of their dead, dressing them and redressing them in everyday clothes, to spend months or years at home before they are ready to pass on to the afterlife, would be horrified at the thought of her body given so little attention.

We chose a brown jumper, with some jewelling around the top, and an easy pair of trousers. The nurses brushed Mum's hair, and wrapped her back up in the fluffy yellow blanket that our children had bought her only six months before for her seventy-eighth birthday. We talked about Mum's laughter and her general openness, and then unexpectedly the nurse who had spent most time with her asked to see the mulberry tree that Mum would finally rest under, as dust and bone. We walked to the bottom of the garden and took it in, the vastness of the tree, the rootedness of Mum's dying place, her home.

She had chosen well.

The nurses told us that there was no rush in organising for Mum's body to be taken. Slightly disassociated and possibly wanting to eradicate all memories of Mum's illness and decline, we paid no attention. At 5pm the funeral directors, a duo in black and institutionalism, came to collect her. Though of course the attendants were not rude, or untoward, there was a distinct difference in their demeanour: upright, doing a job; the sentiment of the nurses – that human knowing – was absent. Here was a patter, 'Sorry for your loss,' and let's get on with it. Before we had had time to take in the strangeness and uncomfortableness of death, Mum was leaving our house for the last time, body in a casket covered in a hideous deep red velvet cloth. This was a moment that I hated.

The nurses had been wise to tell us there was no rush: we had only stayed with Mum for several hours before she left. It was not enough time to take in the enormity of someone having died before and with you. We have this habit of hurrying pain along: and here Dad and I were guilty of just that. In the hospice setting, too, bodies are often removed with some degree of swiftness, efficiency unless otherwise requested. It is an odd approach, given that in many parts of the world in the period of time before burial, family and friends may keep a constant vigil over the body in the home, giving mourners time to travel from further away. Rooted also in superstition, a vigil might once have kept the body safe from ancient dangers such as body snatchers or evil spirits.

At one point, early on in my life as a psychotherapist in palliative care, a member of the nursing team from the Congo had come to meet with me on her induction. She was curious about the work I did, then stated assertively, 'We would not need you in my village.' I was curious about this, and she told me about the way that mourners grieved together, collectively, around the body for days and days and that emotional support was implicit in such acts: far from the often alienated fragmented globalised families and communities we have created in the Western World, this approach may well have circumvented the need for us psychotherapists of grief.

For Dad and I our only option to see Mum again was to make the visit to the funeral director's private viewing area or the 'chapel of rest'. We were in two minds, both agreeing that there were advantages and disadvantages for both; one thing we agreed on was that the thought of Mum – who had had a fiery, warm heart and temper – in a cold fridge, with unfamiliar figures attending to her corpse, filled us with real dread. We never went.

The experience of grief seems to be unique to every one of us: there may be times of overwhelm followed by extended periods of resilience; for some the capacity for joy can still be found in the rustling of trees and in the laughter of children; for others a darkness may descend and the empty space of the absent person is felt acutely in the physical body. We know that grief can manifest itself somatically as well as cognitively and behaviourally. There can, for example, be digestive disturbances, faster palpitating heartbeats, headaches, and insomnia. An all-round upheaval to the psyche and soma. Clients often report new health concerns; a fear about their own mortality and appointments to GPs might increase in the period of intense grieving.

None of us know where grief will take us, and what we might learn about ourselves and the depth of our feelings – from love and gratitude to devastating sadness or a raging sense of injustice. The abruptness or traumatic nature of a death; the acceptance of the dying person and their capacity for letting go; the nature of the relationship (one founded on tricky attachments or on a more mutual sense of wholesome recognition); the care received by professionals or not – all of these things will have an impact on the grieving process. What may be common for all of us, no matter how able we are to journey through the everyday, is that we might notice at base a certain fragility that lurks in the background. And yet it is in this fragility that we may also become aware of our sensitivities and that of others. We might see clearly people's ability to care, and of course those less able to do so. It is, however, perhaps in this encounter with fragility that we discover a more genuine site of love. Not a romantic love or one predicated on giving and taking, but rather a stance of generosity towards one's vulnerabilities, towards the vulnerabilities of others and also towards their differences and their freedoms. If we are able to let go of one human being in our lives whom we have loved, in a finite sense, to death, then perhaps we are now more able to relate to everyone in our lives with concern but without expectation. That is not to say that we put ourselves in harm's way, but rather we become more cognisant of where to place ourselves in relation to others. In grief we now see clearly who is able to give care freely and who isn't, and yet somehow it might just be possible to find an inner strength in this process of awakening to the realities of life's asymmetries.

What ifs

When someone we love dies, no matter how good the relationship, most of us will experience moments of doubt and self-questioning. We might wish that we could repeat certain situations, go over them again with fresh eyes; we might wish that we could change a parent's treatment plan or read their favourite poem one more time before all hearing is lost. In a marriage, we might wish we had noticed those small clues – at least at a more conscious level – that gave us a deeper understanding of our partner; the needs which perhaps they themselves had never managed to articulate in words. As a parent, we might wish we had dropped down to our knees and rolled play-dough more; cuddled more; danced outside more to the made-up tunes of our children. These *whys* and *what ifs*, regrets, are akin to what Kubler-Ross (1969) might describe as 'bargaining' – going over old ground to see if perhaps there were different possibilities. As a psychotherapist I know all this, I understand that we can find irrational hooks for regret, and for our sadnesses: it is the pair of slippers that I bought my mother for the mock-up Christmas we had had together, before that fateful Boxing Day, which takes me to the place of deepest regret. How did I manage to buy her slippers that did not fit her feet? Why didn't I take them back and let her make a snip in the fabric? Did I not value her as much as she valued all of us? Did we let her make do? And, then, worse still, the thought I most wish to avoid, *did we let her die too easily?*

Writing beautifully about the sudden death of her father in *H is for Hawk*, Helen Macdonald (2014) uses the natural world as the metaphorical site of her grieving, the churning and raking up of memories that often plague the bereaved:

> The archaeology of grief is not ordered. It is more like earth under a spade, turning up things you had forgotten. Surprising things come to light: not simply memories, but states of mind, emotions, older ways of seeing the world. (p. 199)

Grief brings with it also the clarity of retrospect and provides us with a lasting lesson: that in our daily lives we are often so very absent from the content of each moment. We are not quite attentive or present enough to the tiny micro-interactions of communication; we resist being as curious towards others as we can.

But no relationship is perfect; we might just hope to achieve friendships, partnerships, parent-ships that are good-enough: enough care, enough responsiveness, in which both parties at least feel valued and are able to emerge as fully as possible. In grief work, as therapists, our role is perhaps to sit with the *whys* and *what ifs* of the bereaved person, to listen to their *should haves* and *would haves*, and to work through the guilty traces of any ambivalent, difficult feeling they may have had. But it is also to notice with the grieving person where the love once lived, where the moments of joy, calm, excitement, playfulness, laughter existed so that they are able to take it back home, into themselves and into their lives. This is not to say that the pain of absence dissipates but rather that, in the absence, perhaps, and sometimes with help, a beautiful seed of memory can begin to grow and to restore enough hope that a new day can be lived. Viktor E. Frankl (1946), author-psychiatrist and father of logo therapy, who spent three years during World War II in Auschwitz, Dachau and other concentration camps, writes:

> Emotion, which is suffering, ceases to be suffering as soon as we form a clear and precise picture of it. (p. 82)

His theories are based on brutal, inhuman experiences of starvation, of constant threats of psychic and physical obliteration, coldness and cruelty, yet faced with this extremity he made remarkable attempts to hold on to meaning, to find ways to continue to understand the human condition with as much empathy and wisdom as he could. This is not to say that grief can be compared to an experience such as Frankl's but it is to say that grief, as Freud clearly hypothesised through his discussion of melancholia, has a way of emptying out both the world and the ego of goodness. It is perhaps, then, the therapist's job, when encountered with human bleakness, to ensure that, without making trite reassurances, the good stuff is also kept in mind where possible so that a whole picture of each relationship and individual is available.

The Paradoxical

Grief also has a curious way of forcing us into living with an even clearer awareness of life's paradoxes – and of course this is not the case for everyone since the experience is individual – but sometimes, in my own life and in the words shared by those I work with, I notice an acknowledgement of the way that grief plunges us into the depths of who we are yet at the same time feels daily so very close to the surface. In the numbness and shock of loss, there can also be a strange realisation that you are living each day in a sort of emotional technicolour where each small expression of other people can be felt more acutely, for good and for bad, and in turn you see your own response and the way you can be touched by someone else. And so this is perhaps the sense of being present that we begin to learn following someone's death, a learning that comes from the question, 'Why didn't I notice these things before?' This can be a time when a sense of the sheer impact of the relational, this vast psychic resonance field, comes into fuller view. I am reminded of the many grieving widows who have shared with me their increasingly observant stance towards the world:

Her life has started to find new energy so she says that perhaps it might be time for her to venture forth into new experiences and to say goodbye to her therapy space. She talks about her walks outside in nature, the way she could see that life continues to have meaning for her, in its most simple form. The room fills with her simultaneous excitement and deep sadness at leaving. Making a move to make contact with her, as she faces another – albeit easier – ending, I say, 'We will both be glad that you are ready to let go of our time together, and also we'll both

be sad.' And somehow it is in these moments of paradox
that our capacity for human contact feels real, genuine
and loving. This, let's say, is both the learning and the
dislocation that can sometimes, not always, be found in
grieving and grief work.

While human contact can help with grieving, picking friends and family wisely who don't shy away from pain, it is also important to develop a capacity to be alone (Winnicott, 1958) and to give some space to yourself, to process the loss and to relearn how to live with yourself, to develop your own interests. Sometimes in relationships we are so bound and entangled with others that we can lose ourselves and our own needs: this is not uncommon in very long marriages where capacities and skills are inadvertently, and without thought, located in the other, the functional or emotional roles clearly demarcated. Some time to ponder these kinds of enmeshments and to unravel them, psychologically and practically, can sometimes help.

Stephen Seligman (2007) discusses the possibility of developing more adequate processes of mentalisation in some clients following a difficult grief reaction. Mentalisation refers to an emerging mental capacity, a crucial process in development where the child comes to understand that his or her sense of 'objective' reality is nonetheless a personal experience, coloured by whatever might be going on inside, and that the objective reality of others may take on an altogether different hue. This revelation leads to a recognition of his or her own sense of subjectivity – and, importantly, of the subjectivity of others.

By theorising about one's own mind, we begin to have a sense of the theory of many minds, a recognition and tolerance for other thought processes and perspectives. Seligman's (2007) point is that grief, following painful separations, can propel people into making more space for excavating their own minds and the realities and intentions – the minds and subjectivities – of those who have died. He states:

> [H]aving one's own mind is both a source and an outcome of the often painful, but potentially exhilarating process of becoming available to other people, to one's own history and interior life, to one's voice and one's actual body, and consequently of life's opportunities and pitfalls. (p. 342)

Beyond grief, of course, we need to develop our own minds and have a sense of the stance we are taking towards others and towards the world so that we are able to distinguish between what is meaningful to us and what we may consider vacuous. There are so many competing forces and ideologies external to us; without a well-developed mind of our own we may become subjects of Althusserian interpellation, following ideas and cultural trends that bring us into tension with aspects of ourselves we struggle to get to know yet which keep manifesting themselves in the symptoms of existential discontent.

Psychotherapy in palliative care often involves working with people to rediscover and to become curious about their own minds, and relatedly to make sense of their lives, as they are now. Seligman (2007) points out that 'making meanings that make sense are a crucial aspect of feeling secure in the world'. (p. 324)

Creating meaning, the process of co-construction, is part of the daily work of therapists and their clients. Evidence might be presented in sessions, for it to be rebuked or, alternatively, taken in to be modified slightly by the client who gradually gains confidence in becoming the author of their own story, an equal, well-equipped meaning-maker in the room. It follows sometimes that this process of sharing meanings alerts people to aspects of their lives that no longer provide them with fulfilment and new meanings emerge upon which people wish to hook their lives.

Nature's Medicine

As well as giving some thought to meaning-making and to the fabric of past relationships so that some disentangling might follow, there are more embodied responses to grief – outside the realms of the therapeutic encounter – which can very much offer some respite from the heaviness that can set in.

Freud once said something along the lines of 'flowers are restful. They have no conflicts or emotions.' We might imagine that when Freud lost his daughter, Sophie, to inter-war influenza he experienced the depth of grief that only parents who lose their children know about. It made him reassess his theories on mourning and melancholia, and he began to acknowledge that the emptiness and pain of loss may never be filled or worked through. We might imagine that in these times of agonising heartbreak, and the numbing paralysis of his daughter's absence, he sought some peace in nature. Who knows?

But in my own grief and in the work I do with those processing their own endings, or the endings of people they have loved, some respite can be found in nature, a seemingly therapeutic realm that comes without the heaviness of thought and words: a trickling stream, a walk among wild grasses and flowers, the crashing of sea, the waddling of baby ducks... all of these moments reconnect us to something larger than our individual selves and our experience. We find that life has value simply because it is; because there is existence, and that existence holds within it a simple beauty.

In grief there is some understanding that movement, exercise also helps with shifting us out of a focus on loss into states of greater restoration. If we also move outwards into nature perhaps the movement – at least momentarily – takes us out of the repetitive thoughts, offering a small break, often much needed, from our internal worlds. We can release tears and we can release ourselves from the tight grip of a controlled smiling face: we can be the storm, the wind, the stillness. Much research (Kuo, 2018; White et al, 2019) supports the view that nature is good for our mental well-being: anecdotally, I know this to be true.

> She is ill at ease in the counselling suite, a closed door reminding her of years of punitive treatment as a child and the room in which her mother had tragically died. Sessions move outside onto a bench, surrounded by woodland: the hood she covers her head with comes down, body once so tense takes on greater fluidity; she imagines that she can talk safely because only her therapist and the trees can now hear her...

Slowing the Pace

In line with the notion of an over-controlled grief response, possibly related to avoidant styles of attachment patterns, people can become overly busy: a manic performative defence towards pain. As Melanie Klein notes, in her seminal paper 'Mourning and its Relation to Manic-Depressive States' (1940):

> The fundamental difference between normal mourning on the one hand, and abnormal mourning and manic-depressive states on the other, is this: the manic-

depressive and the person who fails in the work of mourning, though their defences may differ widely from each other, have this in common, that they have been unable in early childhood to establish their internal good objects and to feel secure in their inner world. They have never really overcome the infantile depressive position… It is by reinstating inside himself the 'good' parents as well as the recently lost person, and by rebuilding his world, which was disintegrated and in danger, that he overcomes grief, regains security and achieves true harmony and peace. (p. 369)

It is the case that sometimes when we are grieving we can distract ourselves by doing and doing and doing more; sometimes this has at its base a healthy commitment to the life instinct. Often people talk about feeling okay because they have managed to get jobs done, tasks completed – the idea being that busyness is representative of coping, of wellness. This also mirrors a societal preoccupation with the appearance of productivity, for some an enslavement to a working life without balance. There might be cause for concern when a client is showing no signs of let-up, a relentlessness to completing tasks, a pushing out of mind any sign of the impact of the loss.

That said, the busyness, this filling of space and time, is understandable because once we do slow down, and find ourselves at rest with the opportunity for reflection, then the images and dreams, those unconscious schema, drift back into consciousness. And we remember… we might remember the last words, the last time he or she opened her eyes, the hardship involved in personal care, the loud booming secretions, blood and pain. All this comes as a surprise when we first take pause, so clever might we have been at disguising our grief in our daily commitment to activity. So while it is invariably hard to do so, sometimes it is quite simply vital to ease up, take a breath, and allow the tears that may have been building for some time.

For each one of us in the family, we have been handling Mum's death differently. My father goes to sit under the mulberry tree regularly. For a man whose rational mind is arguably over-developed, he has been surprised by the way that he has taken to reading signs in nature and in his home – the visits from a robin, the white hairs left behind that fell from Mum's head during chemo – that he feels gives him some indication of Mum's continued presence. He churns over in his memory the earliest memories of their courting, and finds himself saddened that he can't quite pin them down. He imagines Mum telling him off when he has moved the furniture to a place she would have disapproved of; her familiar phrases, ones he had got so used to, when they crossed certain junctions in the car. He tells me how he wants to come in from the garden, having done a job, having built a memorial to her, the weeping girl statue placed on top, under her tree, to tell her what he has done. No one there. All these small daily encounters they had together, nothing special, just brief fleeting encounters of felt human touch. Gone. What we seek from others, what Benjamin (1988; 1998; 2004) might describe as the dynamics of recognition, this is what Dad is looking for – a form of mutual recognition where we move apart in order to come back together, a place in which difference can be tolerated, and separateness survived without a sense of threat. This in some ways seems to sum up what became the gentle existence of my parents.

But with this piece of his life missing, my father is nonetheless able to draw on his own coherent sense of self. He, in Winnicott's terms, goes on being. We might imagine that something in his love relations, early on and/or compounded by his relationship with my mother, has provided him with some sense of ongoing ontological stability and structure from which he draws some strength. And so, while he may dream of Mum, or be interrupted by her present-absence, particularly late at night and/or in the early hours, he also takes walks, writes poems, buys our children presents, makes contact with family, and watches a great deal of rugby. For Dad, as he writes, becomes more cognisant of all that he has lost, aware on some level of his continued object-seeking behaviours:

> I felt in some magical way
> I would find you there,
> Sighting the lost earring
> Beneath your favourite chair,
> Your dark glasses, strap loose
> And curled, a half read book
> Abandoned on a lonely stool,
> A glinting strand of silver hair;
> I faltered through a maze
> Of thoughts, regrets and flecks
> Of pained pathways in the brain
> Oscillating, small bubbles clashing
> And spilling warm tears
> From half expectant eyes
> Of what had been;
> Eyes that must now close
> Knowing always what they have seen. (2019)

Dad has also changed. He has become more open. Our relationship has shifted gear. I can call him now, and he will share how he feels, and listen in turn to my concerns. Before, this would have been my mother's role, but he now gradually finds he has a place in feelings, too. It is, I only imagine, as if he is drawing from his wife, memorialised, internalised, his Jay. Change always sounds as if it is related to a choice, to the new age movement, to the discourse of personal growth. But in grief, change might be imposed, of course, circumstantially through loss. Ann Aragno (2003), writing of her own experience of widowhood, claims that genuine mourning digs deep into profound archaic layers of the personality, and as a result there are existential transformative repercussions. She beautifully reframes the original Freudian paradigm of decathexis from the lost object, a final disengagement that leads to the resolution of grief. Rather, for her, the radical revision of self emerges from a moving – and ongoing – symbolic reconfiguration of the relationship with the dead person, inside the survivor, which both transforms and preserves the delicate and treasured dialogue (with him or her or them) within. It is this capacity for a continued loving internalised reference point that pushes the grief-stricken to living more lightly and generously, foregrounding love over those more difficult feelings associated with grief. It takes time, of course, but herein lies the transcendence of loss through internalisation that may emerge after a laborious and painful process that begins with the shattering of our earlier certainties. Sometimes my father does just this.

His grief though is different to my own because at the age of eighty-four, Mum's dying forces him more urgently to examine his own mortality too; and the possibility of his own unbecoming as he ages each day. We barely speak of this, apart from those moments where he has found himself beset by some sense of anxious, looming existential threat – the fear of choking or of developing strange growths on his body. And so we think about how hard grief is to swallow, and how frightening it can be. He breathes, and goes on.

Childhood grief

For the children, life focuses on play and friends and made-up words and dance routines. Sporadically, there are tears. My son tells me that he misses 'Mama Joyce'. I ask him what about her does he miss. 'Her big plump cuddles, Mum.' He cries, and then finds a warrior figure on the floor and battles with his grief temporarily.

My daughter, older and apparently wiser, hurts with impending adolescence and the desire to challenge her parents without the backing of her soft grandmother, who always took her side. Mama Joyce is missed at bedtimes, storytimes. Mum is a consistently supportive object, a counter to the rules that her parents might attempt to set. 'Mama Joyce would have done this; would have done that.' And so we have her with us, guiding us – a sort of overarching matriarchal container with whom we are still in dialogue.

Only last week, we were snuggled up on a single bed, and an unexpected conversation about regrets came up. My daughter asked her brother if he had any. 'Yes,' he had said. 'I regret not having visited Mama Joyce more when she was dying.' 'I have that regret,' says my daughter, 'and that I didn't cuddle her more,' which in fact she did. A lot. We talked about getting close to dying people, how hard it is, how they would have preferred to remember Mum, what she would think of them, now, a few months on since she has died. Then regret turned to laughter, as we remembered her squeezed into our battered, tiny car, driving around country lanes, lost, on one of our short breaks. The laughter subsiding, my son announces that he will be Mama Joyce now, and he opened his arms wide for cuddles. How grief moves about for children.

Over Christmas, I was given a psychology game from a friend, and the children were intrigued. We opened the envelope, one of those which answered 'who are you?' according to the house you chose. In it were drawings of several house types, the idea being to choose the house that most appeals to you. Our children were over the moon, this seemed like fun: my daughter chooses a mansion, ostentatious, out there; my son a home altogether more frugal, on stilts, in a quiet place. His reads something along the lines of: 'When you don't get what you want try not to let it lead to psychic loneliness or anxiety.' It's all seemingly a bit heavy and abstract now for children, and tears come.

I am concerned, imagining that his tears are about loneliness or anxiety, and ask. I am wrong, as mothers often are. 'It's the bit about not getting what I want.' We discuss the disappointment and anger that might ensue when a toy or an outing is not forthcoming. Wrong again. 'It's not that,' he says, 'the one thing I really really wanted was that Mama wouldn't die, and she did.'

It strikes me that, though it's uncomfortable and unexpected when fun turns to sorrow, this was an extraordinary opportunity to understand the reality and complexity of childhood grief, pain and sadness: not only in fact was this about the absence of his cuddly and committed grandmother, but his expression of sadness was also about the disappointment of magical omnipotent thinking failing – and what a difficult reality this is to assimilate; a dawning that we cannot control all eventualities (as we might have been able to do with a relatively available maternal breast).

A difficult life lesson such as this one, about having to bear frustrations, and having to let go, is nonetheless part of our overall learning and a tricky way into self-containment; and something we are more able to survive when our formative experiences involved a loving present consistency.

Yet this interlude was also about sharing our complexities, no matter the age, and having the courage to do so. In sharing with trusted others, we may come to a place of increased solidity, aware of all those lovely, contradictory bits that make each one of us so unique.

Children also take their emotional cues from their parents, and it is no different in grief. An emotionally brittle family culture will generate emotionally guarded responses, angry parental grievers, angry children and so forth. Sometimes children also take up the care-giving role in relation to a grieving parent, masking their own pain and splitting off their own vulnerability in order to support that person who also needs to support them. Children shift and change, demonstrating exciting skills and different behaviours as they age. As well as learning and growing, new anxieties emerge at each developmental stage. In relation to grief, then, a child of latency years is likely to process grief differently to an adolescent in the grip of separating and individuating, who may have withdrawn from a dying parent or even attacked them at their weakest. In cases like this, a great deal of grief work may follow or be necessary. Like for adults, an acknowledging empathetic other is an important supportive presence for a grieving child – someone who makes room for his upset and provides a place available where he does not have to be so strong.

And yet on the day that we sprinkle Mum's ashes under the tree it was clear that the children had a greater bounce-ability, or resilience, than we adults. My husband cracked as he said a few words about how Mum had welcomed him into her home without judgement right from day one. We read aloud one of her poems, which speaks of her enduring, it seems, acceptance of death:

> There is one day
> When I shall not see
> The white-limbed blossom
> Of the spring green trees;
> No longer seek
> Gratuitous thrills
> Of the easy-going
> And its casual comfort.
> So much is the beauty
> Of my moving world,
> Of the cladded clouds
> And their soft assurance;
> Reluctant when leaving,
> I shall still offer my thanks. (May 2005)

Dad concluded our intimate ceremony with Louis MacNeice's 'Sunlight on the Garden', whose words, 'Glad to have sat under thunder and rain with you' he has now engraved on a wooden bench by the tree. We drank sparkling cider; Fearghas and Eloise said some rhymes, and designed slate hearts to place upon the tree. 'May nature be with you, Mama.' 'You are the best storyteller ever, Mama, we really miss you.' Matter-of-factly they asked if the white ashes were Mama's bones or even her skull, and ran off to play badminton as the adults stayed together and fleshed her life out in greater detail.

Seven months have elapsed since Mum died. There are times when I forget and go to pick up the telephone to tell her something she would have loved to have heard and I would have loved to have shared. I miss her combination of softness and the way she could make a strong stand against any sense of injustice. I miss her laughing which was so loud. Now that she is dead I even miss all those minor irritations: the way she would make the noise of an incompetently grazing gazelle whenever she had a blocked nose; the way she repeatedly told me how to use my own oven when she visited; tried to get me to brush my hair. And so in her absence there is this profound realisation that it really is worth developing tolerance towards others when they are alive, to tread through life with compassion, not a wet, sloppy kindness but with a curious 'ordinary, unsentimental kindness' of the sort Adam Phillips (2009) might describe, that allows you to hold on to your own integrity while simultaneously accommodating many of the fault lines in others.

Seven months on, my friend at the school gate whose father died, only weeks after Mum, is also living her life and laughing still. Seven months on Dad and I speak almost every day, a dyadic little support unit. Seven months on, as I was charging to pick the children up, a mother whom I know vaguely stopped me, her own mother trying to live as well as possible with cancer. 'I have been meaning to tell you,' she says, 'I keep wanting to stop you but didn't know how. Your mum, three years back at one of the carol services…' I can see she is a little nervous about bringing this up. 'I had a newborn baby and my mum was struggling with cancer. I was all alone and broke down in the service, crying by myself. Your mum moved over to me, and pulled a handkerchief from her sleeve, and offered it up. She sat next to me the whole service so I wasn't there with all of that alone. I wanted you to know. I really did. It's those little things that kind people do for other people. She was one of them.'

And it was not so much the kind act that managed to stir up that heavy sense of grief in the thick walls of my throat, but rather that detail of the handkerchief being drawn, magically, from Mum's sleeve. Those handkerchiefs came everywhere, a very real representation of Mum, who was seemingly always to the ready of noticing other people's need or vulnerability; because – as a determined survivor – she knew so much of her own.

Creativity and grief

Grief hollows us out. We weaken. It is in times of grieving that Murray-Parkes and Prigerson (2010) suggest that we are uniquely open both to the help and to the harm of others: experiencing a death leads to heightened sensitivities, and how could this not be so? Whenever a love tie is cut a series of emotional and behavioural adjustments are set in motion: we may become protective, disorganised, busy, and yet we can also open up, soften, empathise, laugh more.

Today, several days after my birthday, as I went to retrieve my coffee cup, the delicate handle broke and I wondered just how we all manage to handle loss... this little breakage, a kind of symbolic interruption to our daily routine, stopping us in our tracks, a momentary pause for thought. Like the cup, we continue to function with a small piece missing. We do handle grief because we have to, choosing not to sink into the cold ground of the dead (as some have been known to do), and more importantly because we want to: grief is as much a part of life as the joy of love. It is love that we need to hold onto, if we possibly can: what more powerful driver of life can there be?

Though the hole of loss, an emptiness, continues, most of us also open our eyes, and hearts, enough to see some growth around this space of absence; unlike an empty can thrown out to fester, we are not static and inanimate. We can change: perhaps we recycle, refashion ourselves, and accept who we have become. When we write about the person who has died and tears come, blotting the ink in front of us, it may blur the words, making them messy, but the stream of sentences carry in them a sense of love that cannot be wiped away. Grief demands forms of expression that somehow convey the unspeakable. Art, writing, creativity help us on our way through loss, this great abstraction strangely – and paradoxically – embodied in our being.

As Philippe Besson (2017) writes in his shatteringly beautiful depiction of the love between men and the finitude of a lover's death:

> I discover the pain of missing someone... perhaps writing is a good way of survival. A way of not forgetting the ones who have disappeared, of continuing a dialogue. (p. 37)

Perhaps we never want to say goodbye to those we love, and yet sometimes the strength to grant them leave is the kindest act, one which allows a dying person to find a peace in parting. And while the memories of the dead come into view at different times, focusing and blurring and back again, so we are left with this new form of life-space, one that is permanently changed and changing, which forces us to reassess the very picture of our everyday.

Grief gives us a different outlook. The lens has changed. Even political events are understood differently. On December 12 2019, almost a year on from Mum's initial seizure, Boris

Johnson wins the General Election. Many of us working in health and social care are angry, frightened, in disbelief. In *Politics, Identity and Emotion*, Paul Hoggett (2016) notes the oscillations and links between grief and grievance, the latter a response to the hurt of experiencing a loss, or an imagined one. Yet it is grievance that leads to a sense of agency, and a shift in subject positions. Grief and relatedly grievance, both examples of collective emotional unpredictability, are, so Hoggett argues, also imbued with possibility, and an outcome of more creative, more integrated modes of thoughtful, political action.

Psychotherapists are generally concerned with individual grief reactions, but my point is this, that grief and grievance, the pain and hurt of experiencing a death of someone close, may lead to a changing, (re-)emergent identity and an oscillation between different emotional and subjective positions. It is for this reason that the mourning period can be filled with confusion and self-questioning. Irving Leon (1999) claims that death shakes the cohesion of the self, particularly for carers of people who are dying and who have been alongside the gradual incohesion of the declining body. For Leon, creative artistic processes, the writing of poetry for instance, may undo or at least repair some of the narcissistic injury – this unhinging – that bereavement may evoke. It stands to reason, perhaps, that the final artistic product returns some semblance of cohesion to the artist, or writer, musician or poet. It is to some extent possible that, in writing about my mother's death and in giving thought to the many experiences of agonising pain and loss, grief and sadness, which I am touched by in the intimate relational work I am privileged to do, a certain degree of overarching structure returns to me, a cohesion, part-imagined of course, that is nonetheless woven together with a multiplicity of human fragments.

Dad and I talk on the telephone, as Mum and I used to. One day, I will feel compelled to record his voice, to capture this closeness that has grown in the space that my mother has left us with. A year has passed since he chased the ambulance, with Mum in it, not knowing where its destination would be. He tells me how this haunts him: it is not uncommon to relive the memories of distress vividly, a series of unimaginably difficult firsts. He remembers the sounds that came from Mum, the yelping and crying out, the awfulness of misrecognising 'my wife'. He considers how frightened he can be when these particular thoughts spring back into consciousness and links it to his own sense of vulnerability and helplessness, the shock of having no control at all.

He tells me, as I come to the end of trying to capture this one story among many from people affected by brain cancer, dying and death, that 'it is so good that we had you with this project to make some meaning of our lives'. However, the meaning of their lives is not in these pages, this imposed meaning of a daughter, the third observational platform in a family of three; the meaning existed long before my birth. Only children are perhaps often tasked with a sort of implicit, and rather responsible, sometimes omnipotent, meaning-making role unconsciously in the lives of their parents. But stripping away theoretical thinking, the psychotherapeutic lens, the pull to analysis and over-analysis, the ending is quite simple: I wish still, as I always will, that my mother was here so she could give all of this her own meaning, her own spin, with that huge, dramatic voice of hers.

FURTHER READING

Appignanesi, L. (2018) *Everyday Madness: On Grief, Anger, Loss and Love*. London: Fourth Estate

Aragno, A. (2003) 'Transforming Mourning: A New Psychoanalytic Perspective on the Bereavement Process.' In *Psychoanalysis and Contemporary Thought*. 26 (4), pp. 427–462

Becker, E. (1973) *The Denial of Death*. New York: The Free Press

Besson, P. (2019) *Lie with Me*. London: Penguin Books

Bion, W. R. (1962) 'The Psycho-Analytic Study of Thinking.' In *International Journal of Psycho-Analysis*. 43, pp. 306–310

Clark, D. (6 February 2018) 'Focus: A Moment for Death and Dying.' Available at Discover Society, https://discoversociety. org/2018/02/06/focus-a-moment-for-dying-and-death/18

Clarke, R. (18 January 2020) '"How to live and die well": what I learned from working in an NHS hospice.' In *The Guardian*. Available at https://www.theguardian.com/books/2020/jan/18/ all-that-is-good-in-human-nature-is-here-rachel-clarke-on-life- and-death-at-her-nhs-hospice

Crociani-Windland (2013) 'Old age and difficult life transitions: A Psycho-social Understanding.' In *Psychoanalysis, Culture and Society*. 18(4), pp. 335-351

De Hennezel, M. (1997) *Intimate Death: How the Dying Teach Us to Live*. London: Warner Books

Didion, J. (2005) *The Year of Magical Thinking*. London: Fourth Estate

Doughty, C. (2017) *From Here to Eternity: Travelling the World to Find the Good Death*. London: Weidenfeld & Nicolson

Ettinger, B. (2006) 'Matrixial Trans-subjectivity.' In *Theory, Culture & Society*. 23(2–3), pp. 218-222

Ettinger, B. (2009) 'Fragilisation and Resistance.' In *Studies in the Maternal*. 1(2), pp. 1-31

Freud, S. (2005) *On Murder, Mourning and Melancholia*. London: Penguin Classics

Froggett, L. (2002) *Love, Hate and Welfare: Psychosocial Approaches to Policy and Practice*. Bristol: Policy Press

Fromm, E. (1942) *The Fear of Freedom*. London: Routledge & Kegan Paul

Gatewood, A. (2010) 'Anticipatory Grief: An Existential Model for Spiritual Care.' In *International Journal of Applied Psychoanalytic Studies*. 7 (2), pp. 143-151

Gawande, A. (2015) *Being Mortal: Illness, Medicine and What Matters in the End*. London: Profile Books

Goldberg, J. (1981) *Psychotherapeutic Treatment of Cancer Patients*. New York: The Free Press

Greengrass, J. (2018) *Sight*. London: John Murray

Green, V. (2013) 'Grief in two guises: "Mourning and Melancholia" revisited.' In *Journal of Child Psychotherapy*. 39 (1), pp. 76-89

Hammond, J. (14 December 2019) 'Joe Hammond's Final Article: "I've been saying goodbye to my family for two years".' In *The Guardian*. Available at https://www.theguardian.com/lifeandstyle/2019/dec/14/saying-goodbye-to-family-motor-neurone-disease-reflecting-on-end-of-life

Hoggett, P. (2009) *Politics, Identity and Emotion*. London: Routledge

James, A. (2012) 'Living with Grief.' In *The Lancet*. Available at https://www.thelancet.com/journals/lancet/article/PIIS0140-6736(12)60248-7/fulltext

Jung, C. G. (1995) *Memories, Dreams, Reflections*. London: Fontana Press

Klein, M. (1940 [1975]) 'Mourning and its relation to Manic-Depressive States.' In *Love Guilt and Reparation and Other Works* 1921-1945. New York: The Free Press, pp. 344-369

Kübler-Ross, E. (1969) *On Death & Dying: What the Dying Have to Teach Doctors, Nurses, Clergy & Their Own Families*. New York: Simon & Schuster

Leon, I. (1999) 'Bereavement and Repair of the Self: Poetic Confrontations with Death.' In *Psychoanalytic Review*. 86 (3), pp. 383-401

Light, A. (2019) *A Radical Romance: A Memoir of Love, Grief and Consolation*. London: Penguin, Random House

Macdonald, H. (2014) *H is for Hawk*. London: Penguin, Random House

Mannix, K. (2018) *With the End in Mind: How to Live and Die Well*. London: William Collins

Meltzer, M. (12 January 2018) 'How Death Got Cool.' In *The Guardian*. Available at https://www.theguardian.com/news/2018/jan/12/how-death-got-cool-swedish-death-cleaning

Murray-Parkes, C. & Prigerson, H. (2010) *Bereavement: Studies of Grief in Adult Life*. London: Penguin Books

Nearing, H. (1995) *Light on Aging and Dying*. New York: Harcourt Brace & Company

NICE Guidelines: End of Life Care, Care of Dying Adults in the Last Days of Life, (2017). Available at https://www.nice.org.uk/guidance/qs144

O'Mahony, S. et al (2019) 'Is Palliative Care Having an Existential Crisis?' Online discussion. Available at https://blogs.bmj.com/bmj/2019/11/12/is-palliative-care-having-an-existential-crisis/

Phillips, A. & Taylor, B. (2009) *On Kindness*. London: Hamish Hamilton

Phillips, A. (2015) *Unforbidden Pleasures*. London: Hamish Hamilton

Porter, M. (2015) *Grief is the Thing with Feathers*. London: Faber & Faber

Ram Dass (2001) *Still Here: Embracing Aging, Changing and Dying*. USA: Riverhead Books

Riley, D. (2019) *Time Lived, Without Its Flow*. London: Picador

Rosenfeld, J. (2 February 2020) 'I'm a psychotherapist, but therapy didn't ease my grief.' In *The Guardian*. Available at https://www.theguardian.com/lifeandstyle/2020/feb/02/im-a-psychotherapist-but-therapy-didnt-help-my-grief-bereavement

Rustin, M., Miller, L., Rustin, M. & Shuttleworth, J. (1989) *Closely Observed Infants*. London: Karnac Books

Samuel, J. (2017) *Grief Works: Stories of Life, Death and Surviving*. London: Penguin Books

Seligman, S. (2007) 'Mentalization and Metaphor; Acknowledgement and Grief: Forms of Transformation in the Reflective Space.' In *Psychoanalytic Dialogues*. 17 (3), pp. 321-344

Stolorow, R. (2011) 'Toward Greater Authenticity: From Shame to Existential Guild, Anxiety and Grief.' In *International Journal of Psychoanalytic Self Psychology*. 6, pp. 285-287

Strayed, C. (2012) *Wild: A Journey from Lost to Found*. UK: Atlantic Books

Taylor, R. (2019) 'The Value of Death: Perspectives on Hospice and Palliative Care Through a UK Lens.' Online

Wood, J. (2019) 'Fragments and Silences: Rethinking Narrative in End-of-Life Care.' In *The Polyphony: Conversations Across the Medical Humanities*. Online, June 2019

Winnicott, D. W. (1962) 'On the Capacity to be Alone.' In *The Maturational Processes and the Facilitating Environment*. London: Hogarth Press, pp. 29-36

Yalom, I. (2008) *Staring at the Sun: Overcoming the Dread of Death*. London: Piatkus

ACKNOWLEDGEMENTS

Almost as soon as Mum was diagnosed with a GBM multiforme, I began writing. It was, for me, urgent, the one immediate access I had to the searing pain of anticipatory grief I was experiencing. She read the first few pages before her ability to process language and make sense of the links between words on a page became completely lost to her. Nonetheless, following those few pages, she unequivocally told me to carry on writing; that she loved what I was writing and that she hoped whatever would become of the silly thing in her brain that 'The Silly Thing', as passages of text, would somehow help others with brain cancer, and other terminal conditions, their families. And the staff teams that support them all. So really the biggest thanks is to my mum, Joyce Jones.

I also have to thank the many men and women in the neuro-oncology and neuro wards in which she was cared for – and who are deliberately renamed or left without name – to ensure privacy. These people treated Mum in the most human of ways, patiently waiting for her to find some way to articulate what she needed or wished to convey, as if they could tell just how important speech had always been to her. I want to thank the palliative care and hospice-at-home professionals, the district nursing team, the GPs – all local to her – who I have also given pseudonyms too, but whose names I have not forget for their consistent ability to care, to attend to, to bring joy into our lives in this most difficult of circumstances. Help like this must be acknowledged, recognised, thanked, over and over again.

Beyond this, I wish to thank all those I work with in palliative care, who, daily, share thoughts and feelings with me and who were always kind during those long months of the silly thing. And to all the people who have sat together with me in different states of unwellness and given shape and body to their own stories; who have found voice in the experience of dying and in bereavement. I have found you all, even in moments of anger and despair, to be generous in the way that learning has been sought and shared. As I have wanted to protect individual experiences, and stories of people I have known, this book only ever provides short vignettes of possible situations, fictionalised, rather than actual, of the kind psychotherapists in palliative care may encounter.

My family: my husband, who stepped in on so many occasions as Mum's cancer shifted and changed, and to our children, who continue to talk about their grandmother, in such an open and remarkably loving way, oftentimes embodying what they felt and miss from her. Dad has been such a support, always, and even now in grief we come close to support one another. There is something about keeping memories alive which allows us the ongoing dialogue with the dead; and sometimes as Dad and I talk it's clear that Mum still belongs to the conversation.

I want to thank Alice Solomons, my publisher, who was encouraging of this project from the outset and who seemed to have an intuitive understanding of what I was trying to write here. Thank you so much. This has meant a great deal. Thank you also to The Brain Tumour Charity for endorsing this book, I can only imagine how delighted my mum would have been; this is fine compensation for the fact that she was unable to donate her brain to medical science as she had wished to do so. From The Brain Tumour Charity itself, 'Today as you read this 14 more people will have died of a brain tumour diagnosis, more needs to be done to double survival. As the UK's foremost brain tumour charity, we are leading the way in fighting brain tumours on all fronts through our work to change these shocking statistics in the future. "Together we will find a cure."'

I have also been incredibly moved by the response I have had from Juliet Rosenfeld, a remarkable writer - who knows grief intimately - and experienced psychotherapist; Pam Firth whose work in the field of palliative care and counselling is well respected; Dr Kerry Jones, academic in end-of-life care with the Open University, and co-founder of Life.Death.Whatever and author, Louise Winter for taking the time to read and comment on the book. The encouragement has been not only a relief to receive, given the sometimes raw nature of the book, but this has also been a real gift that somehow parallels the often generous and supportive world of palliative care.